## ADVANCE PRAISE

*"Powerful and uplifting! Not only can you take the inspiring stories and motivational points to develop your leadership skills, but you will also be able to inspire others to follow your cause. Once you read this book, nothing will stop your progress. Lead or Get Out of the Way! will change you for the better because 'Leaders are not born, they are developed.' Thank you, Gary!"*

ANASTASIA BUTTON, AUTHOR OF *#NEWJOBNEWLIFE*

*"Divergent thinker, executive, and leader Gary Vien expounds on eight powerful principles that will help you conquer life, both personally and professionally, and says it plain—Lead or Get Out of the Way! Change your life and perspective with this fresh, relevant, and fun MUST-read!"*

DR. VIRGINIA LEBLANC, AUTHOR OF *LOVE THE SKIN YOU'RE IN: HOW TO CONQUER LIFE THROUGH DIVERGENT THINKING*

*"Lead or Get Out of the Way! should be at the top of the list for anyone wanting to kick-start, revamp, or push your way to the finish line in leadership. Uncovering eight critical steps to enhancing your leadership style; this book will have your organizational leaders thinking differently about what it is to be a leader today."*

GER CARRIERE, AUTHOR OF *WILD WOMEN: MASTER THE ART OF PRIDE, PRESENCE, AND PRODUCTIVITY*

*"Practical advice with relevant illustrative stories to show how to become the leader you are destined to be. This book is a must-read for anyone, whether just starting out or already climbing the corporate ladder.*

*I encourage every leader looking for leadership insight and ways to get to the next level to read Gary's book."*

STEVE NATHAN, STRATEGIC CAMPAIGNS, AUTHOR OF *BRIDGING THE POLITICAL DIVIDE: CONVERSATIONS ON POLITICAL ISSUES AMERICANS MUST HEED TO SUCCEED!*

*"Gary Vien is a sought-after leader with a natural affinity for showing others how to utilize and hone their leadership skills to enhance significantly many areas of life, from business to everyday interactions that often lead to unexpected opportunities. This book will open doors you didn't even know existed.*

*There is an incredible difference between being a good manager to becoming a well-respected leader, someone who leads by example, without the struggle of continually directing others. Imagine not having to tell people what to do, instead of having people automatically doing what is required, because they want to. This is leadership...this is what Lead or Get Out of the Way! will teach you.*

*Gary's book is a refreshing read on the qualities of leadership and examples of how you can turn up your own lifestyle. This book covers eight critical areas of focus to enhance your traits and become a great leader. I suggest everyone who has a desire to improve their status should read this book, especially if you are in the business world."*

CHRIS DYSON, AUTHOR OF *TARGET PRACTICE: 8 MISTAKES THAT RUIN A LOVE OF THE GAME*

# LEAD OR GET OUT OF THE WAY!

## EIGHT POWERFUL PRINCIPLES TO TAKE YOUR LEADERSHIP TO THE NEXT LEVEL

GARY J. VIEN

An imprint of
Srishti Publishers & Distributors

**Srishti Publishers & Distributors**
A unit of AJR Publishing LLP
212A, Peacock Lane
Shahpur Jat, New Delhi – 110 049
editorial@srishtipublishers.com

First Published in India by Bold,
an imprint of Srishti Publishers & Distributors in 2023

First published by Scribe Media in 2020

Arranged via Licensor's Agent: DropCap Inc.



10 9 8 7 6 5 4 3 2



Printed and bound in India

For Sale in India Only

*I dedicate this book to all the teachers in my life.*

***The first life lessons always begin at home.***

*To my parents—Rogers and Shirley Vien*

*Thank you for my life and the lessons you gave me growing up in a household full of love, integrity, and compassion, along with the energy of five siblings!*

*To my wife—Mary Paula Newmann Vien*

*You have added to my joy, happiness, and life in too many ways to count. You are my best friend, soul mate and the rock of our family. I look forward to growing old with you and fulfilling a promise made years ago—life will always be an adventure!*

*All my love, always!*

*To my children—Kathryn and Laura*

*You are what life is all about.*

*Thank you for the happiness and delight in watching you grow up to be beautiful, caring women. I love you deeply.*

# CONTENTS

# INTRODUCTION

*If your actions inspire others to dream more, learn more, do more, and become more, you are a leader.*

—JOHN QUINCY ADAMS

Three events in my life sum up how I became who I am today. They provided my significant moments of learnings, aha moments, and leadership nudges defining my future.

I will attempt to tie these three events together:

Bookmobile, Little Brown Journal, and Cocktail Parties.

## BOOKMOBILE

Growing up in Middle America, I spent my summers at the pool, exploring the town on a bicycle with my friends, and dreading the mandatory summer reading from our school. I never really liked the latter. We were told "it was good for us," and it was something to "keep our minds growing" as we moved up to the next class. These words went in and out of my ears as a nine-year-old. It was one of the last things I wanted to do, yet it was part of the summer ritual, and everyone in the school was expected to participate.

This year, when the Bookmobile arrived at school, I picked out a biography about Benjamin Franklin. I couldn't put it down. Why wouldn't a nine-year-old boy be fascinated to read about a Founding Father, international statesman and inventor, who once flew a kite in a storm to study electricity? Franklin was a man of great worth and vision and a thought leader in his day.

I was hooked. It was the opening of a new world, where books would be a vehicle for learning, travel, and escape. My mind was a blank canvas, being painted by words and stories of the past. Books introduced new thoughts, principles, and places, transcending time and space.

My father told me to read all I could and become a voracious reader. He encouraged me to enjoy and study books with a variety of genres, to become well-rounded and "interesting"—whatever that meant.

## LITTLE BROWN JOURNAL

When I was twelve, my father gave me a little six-by-nine-inch brown, blank journal. He told me to "fill it up" with things of interest, words to remember, and thoughts to ponder.

What was he thinking! After all, I couldn't help but think I was only twelve. I didn't have any thoughts or know what I wanted to remember. What I did have was a couple of things going for me. I was curious and full of energy. I wanted to know how things worked, how inventors "invented," and what made people act and do the things they did.

What would be the first thing to write about in my new journal? I considered it for a while and looked through other books for inspiration. Most publications didn't start until about the fourth page. They had titles and acknowledgments and a table of contents, of which I had none. With that, I turned to page four and stared at the blank page. Nothing. I had nothing. I closed the journal.

A few days later, I was looking through a book on ancient civilizations. I have always been fascinated by the ancient Greeks and Romans, their architecture, and early history. Something caught my eye, and I instantly knew what I would write on page four.

I got home, picked up the journal, turned to page four, and wrote at the bottom:

***Carpe Diem***

Carpe Diem is a Latin phrase meaning "seize the day." It was first used by the Roman poet Horace to express the idea to enjoy life now because you can't trust much in the future. Live for today.

This expression spoke to me.

It was perfect.

### COCKTAIL PARTY

At age fifteen, my father took me to a rare business cocktail party my mother was unable to attend. He gave me a copy of the day's *St. Louis Post-Dispatch* newspaper and told me to read it and memorize a story from the front page, the sports section, and the local section.

At the party, he introduced me as his oldest son and a freshman in high school. All eyes turned to me.

I looked at each of them and said, "It is a pleasure to meet you. Can you believe the seven innings of pitching by Bob Gibson last night? The Cardinals beat the San Diego Padres 14–3!"

They all began to talk about the Cardinal game from the previous night, and I slowly backed out of the discussion, with an approving glance and a wink from my father.

I learned later my job was to start a conversation, to be present and learn how to speak with adults.

### YOUR JOURNEY BEGINS HERE

These stories are told first to give you a flavor of this book. I am thrilled you have this book in your hands! *Lead or Get Out of the Way!* will provide you with an overview of leadership, told through stories, life lessons, and quotes to guide you on your journey.

Charlie "Tremendous" Jones would say, "You will be the same person in five years as you are today except for the people you meet and the books you read." He also followed up this statement by saying, "Leaders are readers."

There is only one person you have ultimate control over, and that is you. Leaders are not born; they develop and grow from within. Everyone has an opportunity to be a leader, even a great leader if they chose to do so. It takes work, desire, and practice, putting yourself out there to fail and to be successful. Through trial and error and failure come some of the most significant learnings to discover what principles work for you and how you can take your leadership to the next level.

Your time is now.

The opportunities are abundant.

This is your moment.

It is time to read *Lead or Get Out of the Way!*

Seize the day.

## CHAPTER ONE

# SIMPLICITY AND COMMON SENSE

*Simplicity is the ultimate sophistication.*

—LEONARDO DA VINCI

*Nothing is more fairly distributed than common sense; no one thinks they need more of it than they already have.*

—DESCARTES

Why start with simplicity in a leadership book?

Simplicity is something all leaders strive for, and few find. Being a leader is about getting things done through others. It is about the will to take a stand when others won't, and the action to make things happen. Some people are thrust into leadership roles, while others await promotion opportunities.

In my world, everyone is a leader. I hope by reading this book and journeying with me through this discussion on leadership, you will find our time together has sharpened your skills, as you realize the impact you can have in your circle of influence to reach for new opportunities and succeed. You must be the captain of your ship. Just grab the ship's wheel and set sail.

In the hustle and bustle and whirlwind of work and life, simplicity and common sense usually take a back seat. It remains elusive.

Life can be very simple, but we insist on finding ways to make it complicated.

I believe simplicity is genius in a complex world.

## MINIMALIST OR MAXIMALIST?

One would think a characteristic of leadership is to be a minimalist. To cut away the clutter, reduce the "friction" of life by eliminating items which surround you. Believing the "less is more" lifestyle will allow for greater thought, free thinking, and open innovation. The trend over this past decade or two has certainly been to become simpler, to declutter, and to place a higher value on experiences over "stuff."

On the other hand, it is very comfortable to surround yourself and your space with what I call "life moments." Life moments are items which make you smile, remember something pleasant or inspiring, and have sentimental value. Often called "the excess of redundancy," maximalists get energy from their collections by their visual and physical presence. They can be large and bold, filling up all the white space. They place high importance on safety, security, and comfort.

There is no science which says one way is better than the other to determine the type of leader you currently are or will become. One simple test is to look at two surroundings—your kitchen counters and your bathroom. Can you see any backsplash wall space or are they all covered up with appliances, knickknacks or piles? How many items are in your bathroom? A small room, yet anything more than a rug, mirror, soap, and hand towels, tend to lean towards maximalism. You define your living and workspace, which must work for you.

You will find both in the modern and ancient worlds. On the minimalist side, there are Steve Jobs, Leonardo da Vinci, and Henry David Thoreau. By contrast, you can count Thomas Edison, William Randolph Hearst, and Frank Stella as maximalists. All very successful in their own right.

Steve Jobs, the former CEO at Apple, once said, "That's been one of my greatest mantras—focus and simplicity. Simple can be harder than complex. Work hard to get your thinking clean enough to make it simple. However, worth it in the end, because once you get there, you can move mountains."

In the end, it is not about labels, but rather an understanding about who you are, what environment works best for you, and how you can multiply that force to help you reach your goals.

Simplicity does require strong organizational skills. Organizing your workspace and pulling your thoughts and research together so they are easily referenced and accessible will work in your favor. To live in simplicity, you must separate the wheat from the chaff with every item you own and every task you endeavor to accomplish.

You must ask yourself what can be kept and used, and what is thrown away or saved for future use.

It is about distilling the question down to its most essential elements. How simple can it be asked? Then, when you believe you have it, try to simplify it again. Ask yourself, what is the job that I am trying to do? What am I trying to accomplish? What struggles will occur, and what can be done to minimize those pain points?

There is an old saying which says, "The most straightforward answer is usually the right answer." William of Occam explained this in what is now known as Occam's Razor.

William of Occam was a fourteenth-century English Franciscan Friar, who was a significant figure in medieval thought in logic, physics, and theology. In short, he stated, when several explanations are possible, the simplest one is preferred. In other words, the least complicated account is probably the correct one. When given the choice of hundreds of options, it is best to scale these down and look for the most straightforward answers, then remove or "razor" out the more complicated choices in your scenario.

Focus on and use reason with the most common sources of the problem. Your mind will be drawn to explore more exotic ones. Avoid the distraction of searching for alternative truths. How often, when we have an ache or pain, do we reach for "Dr. Google," answer a few questions, and then determine we have the Crimean-Congo hemorrhagic fever? Avoid the over-complication of a situation. As a friend once told me, "Don't borrow other peoples' trouble."

Dr. Theodore Woodward, a professor at the University of Maryland School of Medicine, used to instruct his medical interns with, "When you hear hoofbeats, think horses and not zebras." Good simple advice.

Occam's Razor is not perfect. It is not a law of nature or a form of logic. It can help simplify and compare explanations and probability when faced with questions when searching for the truth.

You can also do what most people do—get more data. You can ask for more reports and spend time on the internet searching for source documents and articles. You can find a seminar or webcast to provide additional substance and thoughts. Also, you can set up a meeting and share this with others and get groupthink on the issue at hand. Alternatively, you can use your experiences, education, and frame of reference to reach a logical and commonsense driven response.

Once the question is understood, it needs to be laser focused, and you need to be ruthless at keeping it as narrow and focused as possible. As soon as you ask the question, others will begin to make it more complicated. They will add new elements, bring in their frame of reference, and start to search for the solution before understanding the question. It is the constant pulling of the reigns early on, which will give you future propulsion.

Many are obsessed with constant movement. Just because you are doing a lot more doesn't mean you are getting a lot more done. Don't confuse movement with progress. Productivity is about completion.

Progress represents the improvement in the activity in which you are engaged. Are you obsessed with "doing something" when you should be working on building time in the day to think, communicating with your teams and prioritizing? Simplifying will make your role easier and harder at the same time. Sometimes, you have to say no.

If you don't get to "it"—be that a chore, completing a project, reaching a goal, or any task you find yourself obsessively working on—what will happen? You can't get everything done at once, so subconsciously you are not doing things you need to be doing. You have found a way to use the time you have and have placed value on the tasks you have decided to do.

There will always be an emergency which needs your immediate attention. The key here is to build in time to handle these quickly. It is a value judgment at the moment.

It all comes down to how we spend our day. There are four quadrants, as described by Stephen Covey in his influential book, *The 7 Habits of Highly Influential People*, falling into two areas—how urgent or not urgent and then how important or not important they may be. I encourage you to pick up this book for a more detailed description of his principles.

The important and urgent always get prompt attention. Items in this quadrant deal with life emergencies, deadlines, and last-minute preparations. There are many urgent and not important things competing for our time, which could be done by someone else through delegation.

Then you come to the not important and not urgent things like time wasters, TV, junk mail, and busywork. Time has a value and is a scarce resource, and these activities are holding you back from obtaining your goals and doing something worthwhile.

The hardest quadrant to live in, and the one you get the most value and self-worth is important but not urgent. In this quadrant, exercise and planning reside as well as building relationships, self-development, and new opportunities. Since it isn't urgent, we put it off. It is here you will see significant leaps in your self-esteem, career growth, and leadership journey.

The choice is always up to you, as you will bounce through all the quadrants many times each day. Balance and intentionality as to where you spend your time will give you the most lift in your career.

## COMMON SENSE ISN'T THAT COMMON ANYMORE

Common sense is the ability to make sound, practical judgments. Being book smart and having common sense are two very different sides of a coin. Some can ace a test and are very bright and academic, and yet they may not know the necessary life skills and activities. The inverse is true as well. Some have incredible instincts and street smarts but have difficulty passing an English or math test.

At times, everyone has lapses of common sense. There is so much information to be found at our fingertips, and it is hard to believe someone can't find an answer to a question. One key with common sense is to think in simple terms and do not overcomplicate the issue. Instead of overcomplicating, try to apply life experiences and general knowledge of the situation. When you think about the question in its simplest terms, the answer usually reveals itself to you. Think Occam's Razor earlier in this chapter, and the simplest explanation is often the correct answer.

One could almost say that common sense is like deodorant. The people who need it most never use it.

By thinking before you act, you avoid falling into autopilot mode and doing the same thing over and over. Situations can change, so you must adapt and look at all the facts. While doing the same thing may be the choice you ultimately go with, thinking opens your eyes to new possibilities and other choices. Continue to search for the truth.

As a leader, you have gained substantial knowledge and skills in dealing with individuals and business situations. You have seen people fail and rise above the others. You have also made some decisions where you would like to have a "do-over." The one thing you have continued to hone is your gut reaction to situations. Learn to trust those intuitions and have a gut check with them. Most times, you have a reason to be concerned, and you must listen to yourself. Sometimes the best questions aren't the ones we ask others, but the ones we ask ourselves.

Your experiences, lessons, and education have taught your brain and conditioned you how to think. Continue to expand your thinking by reading more, practicing more, and reflecting on the outcomes and ways to better the process.

The final point is that all leaders are a product of their own decisions. You are the one who gets to call balls and strikes. The more opportunities you take to make choices are yet another opportunity to hone these skills. The quality of these decisions will continue to grow with a heightened sense of curiosity and the willingness to gather data contrary to the norm. Seek variety. Don't underestimate the power of counsel with other leaders in the organization or trusted advisors and mentors. Bouncing ideas off others will provide a more balanced and thoughtful approach and better results.

By applying the principles of simplicity in your range of skills, along with a heaping dose of common sense and trusting your instincts, the leader will continue to provide more value to the organization, their workforce, and themselves.

## HIGHLIGHTS OF CHAPTER ONE

- Simplicity is genius in a complex world
- Minimalist or Maximalist—which are you?
- Simplicity requires strong organization skills
- Distill the question to its essential elements
- The simplest answer is usually the right answer
- Constant action is activity, not progress
- If you don't do it, what will happen?
- How do you spend your day?
- Common sense isn't that common anymore
- Leaders are products of their decisions

# CHAPTER TWO

# ATTITUDE AND ENERGY

*Nothing can stop the individual with the right mental attitude from achieving their goal; nothing on earth can help a person with the wrong mental attitude.*

—THOMAS JEFFERSON

*It is not what happens to you, but how you react to it that matters.*

—EPICTETUS

*Your positive energy can light up any room.*

—GARY VIEN

A bad attitude is like a flat tire. You can't get very far until you change it.

Attitude is one of the most talked about and most written about topics in these times. When you type the word "attitude" into Google, you get over 425,000,000 results in less than .33 seconds. Why does this topic take so much bandwidth with discussion, comments, and thought? The reality is that attitude is very personal to each of us, and we are all grasping for some understanding and direction on what we can do to be better. In this chapter, we will take some time to unpack how you think about attitude and where to put your energy.

Henry Ford was all about bringing the right attitude to the job. He said, "Whether you think you can, or you think you can't—you're right." He knew the power of self-confidence and surrounded himself with like-minded people. Also, Ford recognized the power of the human spirit and how to bring out the best in the individual.

You have seen this trait in athletes, musicians, and orators. You see them reaching into the depths of their experiences, skills, and prior training. All their energy focused on this one moment in time. Think of Michael Phelps and his determination to set new world records every time he would swim. Picture Prince on the guitar, playing a complex set of chords and making it look effortless. Listen to the words of Martin Luther King Jr., speaking from his heart, touching millions around the globe and being the face of a movement. Each believed in themselves and brought positivity to the forefront of his or her mind—thinking they can, and they must, and they will.

Your attitude says everything about you—who you are, whom you are becoming, and where you are going. For you to become the person you are striving to be, to reach your potential, you must work on the person you see in the mirror every morning. You are the one who decides your fate every minute of every day. You must own your attitude. Your attitude is your decision; it is your choice.

Of course, we are speaking of a positive attitude. Trying to have a positive attitude all the time is a challenging thing to do. It is right up there with trying to climb a ladder as it is leaning toward you and trying to kiss a girl when she is leaning away from you! All very hard to do, and it may not be your natural state of being. If not, then you have deeper issues to wrestle with before you are happy with yourself and able to share your joy with others. Keep finding ways to show gratitude, give to others, and smile often.

Your attitude gives you power over circumstances. There are times when life throws you into a tizzy, giving you the unexpected when you prepared for something different.

The unknown happens all the time, every day. We all learn to zig and zag when we are children, yet somehow we forget this is what life is all about. You must reach down, step up, and make the best of the situation. Things will not always go your way, but it is the path before you.

What would you do if you were driving your car and you suddenly got a flat tire? It is an unexpected inconvenience and can be annoying. So how are you going to deal with it? Many will become angry and scream or cry and talk about how unlucky they are. Others will laugh at their bad luck and begin to decide on what they will do next. Some will start to get the owner's manual out of the glove box and look up "how to change a tire." Some will look at this as another adventure of life and make the most of it. Those who rise above the conflict thrive, and those who succumb to the inconvenience, fear, or pressure, can quickly get swept away by obstacles thrown in their path.

It is important to remember this as you navigate your life. While you can't be ready for all the pies life will throw your way, it is not that you have to prepare for everything, but you must have the capacity to deal with anything. One secret lies in having perspective and the ability to rise above whatever comes your way.

Many predictive studies are trying to correlate a vast number of criteria to determine how individuals become successful. They look at things such as appearance, social and emotional intelligence, physical form, and self-worth. While attitude plays a critical role, there are other attributes, such as having a growth mindset, always willing to learn as a pathway to success, and building relationships. Show me your friends and I will predict your future. Who you are attracts others who are like-minded, shares common interests, and who have the same positive mindset. Attitude attracts attitude.

Positive attitudes and energy are contagious—they go together like salt and pepper. When you smile, your body immediately releases feel-good neurotransmitters called endorphins along with others such as dopamine and serotonin. These relax your body and lower your blood pressure and heart rate. They produce a sense of calm throughout your body, which displays confidence. If you smile at others, they are likely to smile back at you in a reciprocal way. It is much more calming than walking into a room where everyone is grumpy! If you are the leader, how you project yourself will send messages to your team. You want them to be energized and have the right attitude to take on the world.

Ask yourself this question, "If thoughts have energy, what energy are you producing?" Are you spending your time thinking about how much work you must do, you are always behind, and you can't get anything done? Then stop it! Being negative is the essence of the self-fulfilling prophecy. What you think you become. Just think how much you could have gotten done in the amount of time you spent bellyaching about it—time to get yourself off the couch and start doing. Please turn off the TV and spend the few minutes you were complaining about your life and do something to improve it. Start thinking about your plan for tonight, tomorrow, and next week. Take steps with the energy you have and make a positive impact. You will be amazed at how little it takes to get something done and off your list. Moreover, when you do, because of the power of movement and the satisfaction you get from getting something done, you will be more inclined to do more.

You can find inspiration just about anywhere these days. I believe everyone should have an aptitude for social media and should learn as much as possible about how it works, what it can be used for and more. I came across a tweet by Diddy, and it caught my eye and spoke to me. He tweeted, "Your energy introduces you before you even speak." How true is this! Think about when you are in a room and someone walks in who "lights it up" with his or her presence.

## POSITIVE ENERGY PRODUCES POSITIVE RESULTS

There was a group interview going on in a room near my

office. As I walked down the hall, the door opened, and the interviewers were thanking the interviewee. I waited and watched the candidate walk through the lobby and to the double glass entrance doors.

Meanwhile, the interviewers all had their heads out the door watching the candidate. With a puzzled look on my face, I asked my colleague what they were doing. She turned to me and said, "We liked her a lot and wanted to see her walk out the door." I scratched my head and said, "OK." Linda went on to say, "No, you don't understand. How fast someone walks is how fast he or she will work. We are just checking to see if she has any pep in her steps."

This lesson struck me as odd, yet made perfect sense. Next time you are people watching, check out those who are moving fast and those moving slow. You can tell which of your teammates have a mission and the attitude to get the job done and those who are just getting by. Be more like the former.

Believe in the law of the echo—what you project comes back to you. When you are in the mountains and shout "HELLO," the words will bounce around and make it back to you with a booming "HELLO," getting softer each time. The universe is in constant motion. When you speak a sound or think a thought, you send it out in the cosmos. It will return to you after affecting people—bouncing off them—very far away. Some call it fate, some call it providence, and others call it karma. What you send out—positive or negative—comes back to you. By projecting a positive attitude, you will have more goodwill returning to you.

If you ask for help and tell others of your need, you may be surprised at the results. If you need prayer, then pray. If you want to love, then love. If you need help, start helping others. The results of your actions will not be immediate, but they begin to touch others who in turn mention it to someone else, and on it goes. If it is energy you want to attract, then you need to be the energy you wish to receive. The more you give, the more you get. Your positive energy can light up any room.

You are now acutely aware that you are the one responsible for your attitude. You need to be the change if you want to change the world. The responsibility is yours to bring positive energy and a positive attitude wherever you go, in every situation and every opportunity. When you do this, you are taking the leadership reigns of your future.

## HIGHLIGHTS OF CHAPTER TWO

- Whether you think you can, or you think you can't, you are right
- Your attitude says everything about you
- Your attitude gives you power over circumstance
- Show me your friends, and I will predict your future
- Positive attitude and energy are contagious
- Your energy introduces you before you speak
- Positive energy produces positive results

## CHAPTER THREE

# HONESTY, INTEGRITY, AND HUMILITY

*Honesty is the first chapter in the book of wisdom.*

—THOMAS JEFFERSON

*If you tell the truth, you won't have to remember anything.*

—MARK TWAIN

*Work for a cause, not for applause.*
*Live life to express, not to impress.*
*Don't strive to make your presence noticed*
*just make your absence felt.*

—AUTHOR UNKNOWN

### HONESTY

You are your own, individual brand.

No matter how old you are, what position you have, or what you have accomplished, you are the one who created and continues to create the image of who you are to others. Your individual and personal brand is built over time, not overnight. It grows through the sum of all your interactions with others. What they see, how they felt, and what they remember builds or detracts from your brand.

What it all boils down to is you are the face of your business to others.

A great deal of your responsibility will be to hone your attitude and spend your energy in positive ways. When it comes to your reputation, it is an opinion and a belief which others have about you. It is something crafted over time and through continued interaction with someone. It is respect from others, which is earned, not granted. Esteem and respect are fragile, and each needs to be constantly nurtured at every opportunity and encounter. Your reputation takes years to build and seconds to destroy. Once lost, it is a very steep road to regaining a status you once had—though not impossible, and it can be rebuilt over time and through quick, diligent actions on your part.

We all wake up each day, get ready for work, and begin

with high expectations. We are all honest people, and we expect honesty in return. Honesty is appreciated yet can be very challenging. How realistic are you with yourself? Can you be self-critical? We all would like to make changes to ourselves, but are we willing to take the necessary steps which will lead to changes in our future? The thing is, we expect more honesty out of our friends, coworkers, and leaders than we do from ourselves.

We all have that one brutally honest friend. They seem to not have many filters from their brain to their mouth. They make comments which make you cringe and take a deep breath. Once stated, they look at you and say, "What?" They can be very judgmental and see themselves trying to help and talk about the "elephant in the room."

This tactic, in a business environment, is seen as direct—an offensive move to gain an advantage and to position the listener in a defensive mode. However, for someone on the receiving end, this approach may be unprofessional, uncivil, and discourteous. While it can be adequate for laying a position on the table, it creates immediate negative emotions, heightens tension, and makes it more difficult to find a quick solution. I am not a proponent of this strategy. I believe in building relations over time, finding ways to listen and work with others while still focused on the goal and the work to be done.

With ubiquitous social media and the hundreds of ways to express yourself, you need to be cognizant of the raw truth. Your words, even those printed online, have consequences. Whatever you put online, you own. Keep in mind what type of reputation you are trying to build and how your post impacts your brand.

Every time you send a tweet, post on Facebook, upload a picture on Snapchat or Instagram, you are throwing yourself into the wild west of the internet. On the World Wide Web, there are few rules and fewer safe places. With each post, you are sharing with others your thoughts, personal stories, and showing who you are. You are seeding the fields with the essence of yourself. Be prepared for the backlash and think twice before posting.

Anyone in the world can hide behind their keyboard and become a critic. They become instant authorities on every subject presenting every side of every story and then some. Honesty comes from the writer's point of view. You must decide if they are providing any new information or thoughts for consideration.

Words cut deeper than actions. Say what you mean and mean what you say. If you don't have a kind word to say, then don't say anything. It would help if you tasted your own words before they leave your mouth. Harsh words have long-lasting pain. A kind word or a word of encouragement breathes life into others.

If you want to live honestly, then live all the time honestly. Once you begin to tell a lie, you are walking down a dangerous path. It all starts with a single lie. It takes other stories to cover up the first lie. If you always tell the truth, you never have to lie.

It reminds me of a group of four students who left campus during lunch and didn't get back before the next period. When they came into the classroom late, the teacher asked them, "Why are you late for class?" One of the boys answered quickly, saying, "Our car had a flat tire!" The others promptly nodded and agreed. The teacher, not believing the story, asked the boys to come to the front of the room. She gave them a piece of paper and a pencil and told them to go to one of the four corners of the room. She then asked, "On the paper provided, write down which tire was flat."

When you operate in a simple, transparent, and honest way, you gain the respect and admiration of your team and others. Parents, employers, and coworkers want the truth and can handle the truth. It says as much about you as it does about them. If you did something wrong, own up to it. It shows you are willing to learn and grow from your mistakes. There is an expectation of honesty in leaders like you.

### INTEGRITY

Honesty is a building block for integrity. Integrity is the guarantee of honesty and reputation on your internal moral code, ethics, and values.

Your moral code, ethics, and values are the consistent set of rules by which you learned right from wrong, how to conduct yourself with others, and a guideline to live by for a practical and happy life. Most world religions that teach morality believe these morals come from a higher power. Regardless of faith, the idea of morality has similarities throughout the world. One good example is an ethic of reciprocity, also known as "the golden rule"—do unto others as you would have them do unto you. In the same vein, values are those things an individual believes are vital to them and how they are central to who they are and who they will become. Values provide an approach to decision-making with clarity and confidence.

Integrity is not something you display to others, but rather how you treat them tells them everything they need to know. Show respect and empathy with an appropriate conversation, and do not spread gossip or talk badly about someone behind their back. Even small things are essential, like letting a cashier know she gave you too much change back. Following the rules of the road, even when there is no one around. If you are at a function, recognize the staff working the event. Talk to them, thank them if they bring or remove a plate, and treat them with respect. Show some humanity by following the company policies and working when you are supposed to and waiting to socialize, search the internet, or place personal phone calls during your breaks. Inform your team of the direction and expectations, and never take credit for someone else's work.

Keep your word. If you are making a promise to someone, you keep it. Your word is your bond. Words may lie, but personal actions will always tell the truth. When given a choice, choose good. Be consistent in these actions to build character and trust. To build trust, you first demonstrate integrity, sincerity, and reliability. Do as you say or don't say it!

When thoughts of "no one is looking," "I am sure I can get away with this," and "no one will know but me" begin to creep into your mind, they can only get you into more trouble than what it is worth. These words ring hollow in the face of integrity, and you must show the courage to stand up for the truth. You must do what is right, not what is easy. Dependability and reliability are hallmarks of integrity. If you fall, pick yourself up and start again, Renew and recommit yourself.

We cannot become complacent with our ethics, values, and integrity. These are fundamental and core principles for all leaders. We must continue to challenge and remind ourselves of our responsibilities as leaders and to hold ourselves up to higher standards. Leaders must continue to show respect, understanding, and compassion for each other and the workforce.

Abraham Lincoln, the sixteenth President of the United States, once summed up honesty and integrity this way: "I am not bound to be true. I am not bound to succeed, but I am bound to live by the light that I have. I must stand with anyone who stands by right, stand with him when he is right and part with him when he goes wrong."

## HUMILITY

I saw this quote from Timothy Keller, an American pastor, theologian, and author. This thought sums up much about this section:

> "Humility is so shy. If you begin talking about it, it leaves."

Have you ever seen a genuinely humble person talk about themselves and how humble they are? Probably not. After all, it is a contradiction to the highest level! A genuinely modest person would never want to be the focus on themselves in such a profound way. If someone tried to talk about their high levels of humility, they would likely steer the conversation away from themselves and towards others in the room.

Humility is the ability to think of yourself less, and to put others first. It is a tenant of servant leadership at its core by pushing the good of others before self. It teaches one to accept criticism as courteously as we receive compliments.

I had a chance to speak to transitioning servicemen and women at MacDill Air Force Base in Tampa, and found many servicemen and servicewomen practice this servant leadership concept. I am in awe of every branch in the military. Many of the participants spoke to me following my talk of putting their squads first, taking care of the details so their team could be the best at what they were trained to be, and being there for each team member. They also spoke of how leaders ate last and made sure the enlisted were taken care of while the officers tended other duties. The United States military was able to capitalize on humility as a leadership trait and have done it magnificently.

Humility is also about changing your perspective when

given a set of facts by putting the other side first and searching for a win-win scenario. Being able to take a different viewpoint and compare it to yours, and putting people first will strengthen the overall outcome. You do not always have to be right, and it can be helpful to listen and learn from someone else's perspective.

Another consideration is to avoid arrogance. It is too often that a new leader will feel like they have an attitude of superiority. After all, why wouldn't they? They were promoted and given the nod by the company. They were the best candidate for the job. They have to prove themselves because they are better than everyone else and much more significant, right? Unfortunately, this type of thinking can lead to disastrous results in a leader.

There is nothing more disastrous than the combination of arrogance and youth. We sadly see it every day with new supervisors, managers, elected officials, and others. They believe they can come in and change the world; it is their time, and by gosh, do what I say, and everything will be fine. Going down this path is such a slippery slope where there is little traction to pull back on. There is much to lose and little to gain.

Humility is about being honest about your weaknesses and helping others overcome theirs. It is the knowledge that everyone is going through something—a personal illness, a family crisis, money issues, marital problems, car repairs, and others. Showing a bit of compassion and using your listening skills will help them overcome and better prepare themselves to be present when at work or at home.

It is also about learning to appreciate and admire the qualities of others and what they bring to the table. Learning more about the person will allow the leader to determine newfound skills and traits for future projects (which gives them energy), and what they will avoid. It builds a personal relationship between two individuals who are then working towards the same goals.

## THERE IS NO INDISPENSABLE MAN

I had spent ten years working with Six Flags in St. Louis. After I earned my BSBA from the University of Missouri, I applied to become the head of personnel at the St. Louis park. I was turned down for the role. Understandably, this was quite a disappointment to me, since this was the job I had been positioning myself for the past several years. Over the next few weeks, I struggled with accepting the decision and tried my best to process the disappointment.

Thankfully, my story does not stop there. I kept moving and did my best to roll with the punches after what felt like a huge setback in my career. I always had heard that when one door shuts, another one opens. Soon, a new and exciting opportunity came my way.

As a result of the personnel manager transferring from AstroWorld in Houston to St. Louis, AstroWorld was looking to hire another personnel manager to fill that role. The director of administration in Houston, Mike Glennan, who used to work in St. Louis, was the individual who hired me ten years earlier, and interesting enough, would do it again eleven years later. I interviewed for the position and was selected for the job. Problem solved, and I was on top of the world with everything going my way.

A few days later, I received a letter from my father. I opened it and found a note saying,

*"Very proud of your accomplishments and for being my son. Here is a poem you need to read and remember throughout your long career."*

DAD

The poem is called *Indispensable Man* by Saxon White Kessinger, written in 1959. I would highly encourage you to read it several times.

It speaks of humility and understanding oneself and letting the air out of your head just when you are feeling pretty full of yourself. It goes on to illustrate your importance by asking you to put your hand into a bucket of water. When you remove it, the hole remaining in the water is how much you will be missed!

Ouch.

Moreover, it talks about your relationship with others and how we build up our ego when we should focus on doing our best, enjoying the moment and while playing a role for just a while, and not forgetting what is important in life. It ends by reminding you to do the best you can and to be proud of your accomplishments because there is no indispensable man.

Gotcha.

This poem hit me right between the eyes and in the gut. It gave me an insight. I still read it and carry it with me to this day.

Let the air out of your head. Focus on others over yourself. Everyone is going through something. Be better every day. Do your job. Be kind. Have fun.

## HIGHLIGHTS FROM CHAPTER THREE

- You are your own individual, unique brand
- Actions have consequences
- Words cut deeper than action
- Reputation—takes years to build and seconds to destroy
- Live honestly at all times
- Honesty is a building block for integrity
- If you don't want anyone to find out, don't do it
- Your word is your bond
- Humility is the ability to think of yourself less and to put others first
- Avoid arrogance
- There is no indispensable man

## CHAPTER FOUR

# ADAPT, CONTROL, AND SELF-DOUBT

*It is not the strongest of the species that survives, nor the most intelligent. It is the one that is most adaptable to change.*

—CHARLES DARWIN

*Everybody thinks of how they can control others, but rarely does one think of how to control themselves.*

—GARY VIEN

*If you hear a voice within you, say 'you cannot paint,' then by all means paint and that voice will be silenced.*

—VINCENT VAN GOGH

Humans, like all species throughout the world, are evolving and adapting to their environment every day. We do this involuntarily with every breath, with every blink. Our eyes are repetitively scanning the room for shapes, light, and information. Our ears are listening for sounds and translating them into useful data to determine our next course of action.

We use this information to build our frame of reference, make decisions, and to decide whom we interact with every moment. We keep changing, adapting, and learning from everything around us. Each situation is different in the short run. The long game is survival and building upon each encounter not only helps us grow but helps us to thrive.

Charles Darwin's theory of evolution, in his masterful 1859 work, *On the Origin of Species*, is a brilliant and scientifically accepted piece regarding the concepts of natural selection and biological diversity. In short, those who adapt are successful in carrying their traits to future generations.

While working around animal care professionals, I often heard them use an interesting phrase. They would say all animals must do one of three things—adapt, migrate, or perish. This behavior was observable not only in the animals under our care but also the humans who worked for us, and the vendors providing goods and services.

You could see it in the team members we hired. How quickly most were to adopt our culture, and how quickly they picked up the tasks to perform their duties. Once they were on the job for a while, many wanted other responsibilities or wanted to move to another area to learn new skills. For those who didn't want to follow the rules, they had a hard time following instructions and "self-selected" out of the organization to become a guest or customer rather than an employee. The employees make choices in their life cycle—they either adapt to their environment, migrate to another role, or leave the company.

Think about how this applies to businesses. How quickly does your business adapt to a new set of circumstances or changes thrown at it with technology? With the rapid pace of technological development and the ever-evolving landscape, those businesses which last and thrive are the ones who can see a roadblock, a new piece of technology, or a new competitor, and can adapt and change the business to succeed in the future.

The classic example of this is the companies who made buggy whips at the turn of the century. They thought they were in the buggy whip business and failed to recognize they were in the transportation business. How many buggy whip businesses are there today?

We see it play out in the story of the early days of Netflix.

At first, the founders of Netflix tried to sell their ideas to Blockbuster. However, Blockbuster did not see the potential and the way our society and the pace of technology was moving, and they turned down Netflix. We all know how the story of Netflix and Blockbuster ended. Blockbuster has shuttered all but one store, and Netflix is a large company, which has tens of millions of subscribers around the world. Netflix continues to grow into a subscription-based streaming service and adapts by creating original content, production, and distribution. Netflix continues to find ways to be germane in today's world.

With the world in constant motion, we must do the same. You are in control of yourself and your destiny. You control your thoughts, your feelings, and your actions. Doing nothing is not an option! If you decide to do nothing, then this means you are not adapting at an acceptable pace, losing ground and being left behind. Everything changes all the time. Keep improving, keep getting better, or you become irrelevant.

To become relevant, learn to be observant. One easy way to understand the world is to look at it with different eyes. Be curious. Study nature and life cycles. There is a reason for the spring, summer, fall, and winter. How does this apply in your own life, your career, your situation? If you are in the "winter" of your job, then you may want to leap into something better, something which gives you energy, something sustaining. It may be the rebirth you were looking for to reinvent yourself.

One of the most beautiful definitions I have ever heard is for the description of a river. This definition is an analogy for life itself and where we are going. Simply and eloquently, it is "water seeking its own level." Are we not all looking for our place in the world, in the company, in our family? How treacherous the travels would be with waterfalls, fast-flowing rapids, rocks, and deep pools. How calm and peaceful we become when we reach the bottom and spread out to fill every nook and cranny. Occasionally, it takes what seems to be a lifetime to be accepted, to know your place, to become part of the team. Then, we move through evaporation back to the top of the mountain as rain to start anew. Individually, we are all seeking our levels in this life.

As leaders, we need to continually update our mental library of what works and what doesn't. Most of us do this through intuition and the school of hard knocks. It is OK to make a mistake if it is not fatal. Also, an error is only a mistake if you choose not to correct it.

Don't forget the power of opposites as you adapt. If I asked you, "What are your favorite movies," you could tell me the ones you liked, you can tell me the dogs and what not to see, and in the vast middle, are the hundreds that were neither good nor bad. The power of three at work again.

## THINK COUNTERINTUITIVELY

The Royal Air Force (RAF) during World War II had a problem with bombers not making it back to their bases after flying missions over Germany. The planes that made it back were shot full of holes from antiaircraft fire. The RAF knew they had to do something, so they decided to equip the bombers with armor. The problem was where to put the metal plating.

Officers from around the country began to study the returning planes. They made copious notes on where all the bullet and flack holes had penetrated the fuselage and how many holes there were. Holes were everywhere! They understood by adding additional weight and drag to each aircraft meant fewer bombs in the bomber bay. Through their studies, they determined the extra armor would go over the existing holes.

"Not so fast," said Abraham Wald. Abraham was a member of the Statistical Research Group (SRG) during the war, using his applied statistical skills to various wartime problems. He, too, inspected the aircraft and came up with a different answer. The military was inclined to place the armor over the existing holes. They did not have the luxury of inspecting the bombers which were shot down. These planes made it back to the base safely with holes in areas where they didn't need any extra protection. Wald suggested reinforcing the regions in which the returning aircraft were unscathed. Those who didn't make it back were shot in more vulnerable places on the plane than these, and if hit in those areas, would be shot down.

## CONTROL

Here is a fundamental truth—you can't control everything.

You can't.

It is like trying to control a force of nature. You have little chance of holding back the river current. The sun will come up and set each day without your help. Let nature take its course and find ways to multiply this force.

You can't control other people. Everybody thinks of how they can control others, but rarely does one think of how to control themselves.

The only thing you control is you, your feelings, and your actions. It is this self-control which will give you leverage in your life. Begin to harness this power of controlling the things you can control.

You gain control by the thoughts you think, things surrounding you, and the actions you take. Don't let others take control of your views and life through anger, guilt, and emotions. If you do not control yourself, then someone else will control you.

Your mind is one of a kind and the most potent attribute you possess. It takes years of practice to develop self-control, self-discipline, and self-awareness. Your brain works 24/7, even when you are asleep. Sleep is when the brain recharges, re-sorts, and replays the day's activities. Developing these three "selves" will take a lifetime.

To help train your brain, surround yourself with positive images, goals you want to achieve, and the skills you want to learn. If you are regularly playing video games, watching television, or feeling sorry for yourself, then you will get what you are acting out. You will stay in your rut—which is a grave with both ends kicked out—until you hit bottom and decide you want a better life and you want to change.

Ben Franklin wrote, "Moderation in all things—including moderation." This statement can help guide your life. All of us, at times, have taken something to the extreme and have regretted it. How many wasted hours have we used sitting in front of the television, how many "one too many drinks" or "I shouldn't have stayed up this late" have you had? Controlling the peaks and valleys of our lives will help to smooth out the living chapters and make us more productive, feel better, and happy.

If you are depressed or bored, then you have the power to change this. You are thinking inward rather than thinking outward. The fastest way to turn these thoughts around is to do something beautiful for others. Help someone who needs some assistance. Write a note or letter. Hold the door open. Return the shopping cart. Make the world better one action at a time, and your purpose and life will do the same.

The final thought on control after knowing you can't control everything, is sometimes you need to let go. Relax. It will all work out without your input, and that is OK. There is an old Polish idiom, "Not my circus, not my monkey." It may not even be your problem in the first place! Learning how to let go is a significant multiplier of time management, so you can focus on the items in your life that bring more enjoyment and happiness.

## SELF-DOUBT

Have you ever walked into a room or a meeting, looked around at all the talented people and thought to yourself:

- "I shouldn't be here."

- "These people are much better than I am."
- "I feel like a fraud. What happens when they find me out?"
- "Wow, everyone here looks like they really have it together, and I still don't have a clue as to what's going on."

If so, you have experienced imposter syndrome—a phenomenon where, despite all your successes and areas you excel in, you remain convinced you are not deserving of all the attention you are getting. Success and accolades are for others, not you! It is difficult for you to internalize your accomplishments. The situation or circumstances which brought you here, have thrust others' perception of you upward, while you believe you have fooled others into thinking you are smarter than you think you are.

Imposter syndrome is an ordinary wonder by many people who have saved someone's life. The hero feels like they did a small deed, and the press or others blow it out of proportion. "I did what anyone else would have done," and "I was just lucky being there at the right place at the right time" are common answers. They don't see their actions as significant as others. "I was just doing my job."

Imposter syndrome is more common than you think:

- Maya Angelou, an American poet and writer, once

said, "I have written eleven books, but each time I think, 'Uh oh, they're going to find me out now. I've run a game on everybody, and they're going to find me out.'"

- Mike Myers, an American actor, comedian, screenwriter, and producer said, "I still believe that at any time the no-talent police will come and arrest me."
- Albert Einstein, a German-born theoretical physicist who developed the theory of relativity, said, "The exaggerated esteem in which my life is held makes me very ill at ease. I feel compelled to think of myself as an involuntary swindler."
- Even Groucho Marx, an American satirist, said, "I wouldn't want to belong to any club that had me as a member."

There are many ways to get beyond this feeling. First, you have to understand everyone feels like an imposter sometimes and it is OK. Second, this is only a feeling, and others believe in you and want to be in your presence as much as you want to be there. Third, be humble and embrace the adulation with grace and thanks. Fourth, tell yourself you are not a fraud and you are meant to be here. So finally, know everyone else is feeling the same thing, so embrace it and don't let this fear stop you.

As you change your life and develop your leadership skills, another focus must be the ability to change your priorities. By adapting to the world around you, controlling your thoughts and actions can help you realize there is a place at the table for you, and you can hold your head up high. This simple action will change the trajectory of your career and the way you look at yourself.

The extra effort you are making to advance and develop your skills will let you stand out in your field. Your confidence will grow as you stand a little taller and are actively involved in managing yourself.

There is wisdom in a Chinese proverb which asks, "When is the best time to plant a tree?" The answer was twenty years ago. They then ask, "When is the second-best time to plant a tree?" The answer is now.

You have what it takes to be better than you were yesterday.

Don't wait for the perfect time. It will never come.

The time is now.

Start today.

## HIGHLIGHTS FROM CHAPTER FOUR

- Build your frame of reference
- Adapt, migrate or perish
- The world is in constant motion
- To become relevant, learn to be observant
- Be like a river—"water seeking its own level"
- Think counterintuitively
- The only thing you control is you
- Moderation in all things
- Think outward instead of inward
- Learn to let go
- Everyone feels like an imposter, and it is OK
- Don't wait for the perfect time. It will never come. Start today.

## CHAPTER FIVE

# RELATIONSHIPS

*If you want to go fast, go alone. If you want to go far, go with others.*

—AFRICAN PROVERB

*A person who feels appreciated will always do more than what is expected.*

—ANONYMOUS

To lead effectively, you need to win over the minds and hearts of the people you supervise, along with those of your peers and boss. The decisions you make—sometimes on a minute-to-minute basis—must stand the test of time and logic.

Your leadership style must command the personal respect of those you lead. Don't underestimate all the powers of simple courtesy, fairness, and humility. Then build deep relationships, which you will use throughout your career.

There are two very distinct ways to develop these relationships—either you can build them a foot deep and a mile wide or a mile deep and a foot wide. One may prefer to make their friendships somewhere in between, and the difference is very apparent.

If you are building relationships which are a foot deep and a mile wide, it means you are probably collecting business cards and LinkedIn connections, rather than knowing who the individual is as a fellow human. You have so many acquaintances and have little time to make meaningful relationships. You know people all over the country and world, but by name and association only. If you meet again, you have very little to discuss.

On the other hand, if your relationships are a mile deep and a foot wide, it means you have a few or several close friends. You would rather stay with your close friends than take the time to meet new coworkers, classmates, or industry execs. On a positive note, it also means remembering their birthdays, weddings, or other life events of great importance. Knowing their families, where they grew up, and what is important to them, means there is always something to discuss.

In business and life, these two strategies are most effective when blended. Keep the friends of your youth, and grow the relationships inside work and your industry. Take time before meetings to talk with coworkers. You typically have lunch every day, so put your courage on and one day a week, sit at a different table or ask someone or several others out to eat. Discussion and exchange of ideas are where relationships begin and grow.

There is an adage which states, "Show me your friends, and I will show you your future." Whom you spend time with says a lot about you and where you are going. People tend to group themselves with like-minded people. It is also essential to grow your circle of friends to experience divergent thinking and situations. In essence, you are but a network of your relationships.

For successful relationships to take root and grow, there must be an element of trust. Trust is at the bedrock of building relationships. Without it, they cannot flourish and grow.

How do you know if you trust someone? Think about some of your most trusted relationships and try to define what it is that has built this trust. Some of the elements of your trusted relationships may include honesty, believability, and reliability. They may share your same values and have proven themselves in the past. You can count on them being there and work well with their personality and pace. All of these take active participation by both the giver and receiver. Telling someone you trust them builds strong roots which strengthen.

Trust is fragile. It is built over time and lost in the blink of an eye. The loss of trust in someone is disappointing and disheartening. Both parties have to make a conscious effort to repair the relationship, if possible. Remember this, when someone does something wrong, don't forget all of the things he or she has done right. Don't throw the baby out with the bathwater. What may seem to be the simple answer may not be what indeed happened. Talk with them, be open and honest with your observations, and allow them the opportunity to respond. Time heals many wounds. You are the only one who can decide your next steps.

### A SIMPLE HELLO CAN LEAD TO A MILLION AND ONE OPPORTUNITIES

Regardless of what language you speak or how you treat

those you come into contact with, talking to others is common courtesy which will open many doors. You should also be aware of cultural and social norms which may prohibit you or forbid you to use this practice. Follow the guidelines in your own country.

Hello is a universal greeting. I am not suggesting you say "hello" to everyone you pass on the street or in your office. However, given the right moment, it may be fine to "put yourself out there" and begin with a greeting, eye contact, and a smile.

You can begin a relationship in this manner, but to build one, it takes effort and patience, collaboration, reciprocity, and purpose.

In his book, *How To Win Friends and Influence People,* Dale Carnegie wrote: "You can make more friends in two months by becoming interested in other people than you can in two years by trying to get other people interested in you."

This statement is compelling and meaningful. I strongly urge you to borrow or purchase a copy of this book as it is one of the most influential books that has had a lasting impact on my life and I am still using his principles today.

Become interested in the other person first. Ask them

open-ended questions about their life, where and how they grew up, and their likes and dislikes. See what they have in common with you and where some differences are. Learning more about others will bring together lives and build the most robust and rewarding relationships.

### YOU CAN PRETEND TO CARE, BUT YOU CAN'T PRETEND TO BE THERE

Another leadership success trait and one used in building relationships is the art of showing up. You can't lead from behind; you have to make it to the front lines of the organization to show strength, camaraderie, and care.

I heard Brigadier General Thomas V. Draude, a retired officer of the United States Marine Corps, make this point very clear during a talk to our 2003 Leadership Tampa Class. He said while serving overseas in a command position, the vehicles assigned to his battalion were not very reliable and were consistently in the shop. One morning, at zero four hundred, he, alone, went to the motor pool to talk with the mechanics. They all saw him come through the door and immediately jumped to attention. "At ease, everyone," he said. "Show me all of our vehicles in for repair."

The mechanics were very seasoned professionals and knew what they were doing. Draude listened intently, asked questions about reliability, wear and tear, and general maintenance. He engaged them in a conversation to get a better understanding of how they saw themselves as vital to the mission, and the problems and solutions in the current state. He asked them to describe what they saw in the field. They all mentioned one issue—the sand and high desert heat in the oil—and told the general; dependability would improve with more frequent oil changes. Draude listened and said, "Let's get to work."

The mechanics all agreed and thanked the general for stopping by the shop. They were even more surprised to see the general grab an oil filter and climb under a vehicle to change the oil. He stayed there, side by side with his men and women, changing the oil, and getting the trucks ready to be deployed. Four hours later, with plenty of oil and grease on his hands, the majority were completed.

He thanked them for their support and urged them to do whatever needed to be done to keep those vehicles healthy. He also mentioned if they needed some help, to give him a call and he would be right over to change the oil. He was back in his office before 0800.

What do you think was the most relevant and essential job on the base that day? Did the mechanics have a new sense of mission and purpose? Absolutely. General Draude could have heard about the problems, sent his lieutenants to do the job, and went on to other things. He didn't. He knew he needed to raise the profile of this task to mission-critical. He didn't pretend to be there—he was there, getting his hands dirty.

Busy leaders always find a way to make time to care for others, and at times, work side by side.

## NO RELATIONSHIP IS PERFECT

The simple truth is that there are no perfect relationships. You may have, or know of someone who says they have the "perfect relationship." While this may be accurate for a moment, it is wildly off base. Each person in the relationship chooses to focus on the good parts and push down the bad areas of a relationship. Give and take is how relationships work.

Humans are complicated creatures who have their personalities, likes, and dislikes, and can change their minds with the wind. We are fickle beings. There will be good times and bad times, and it is in the bad times that you put some extra effort into the relationship so you can get past the dark clouds of a storm.

If you can spend seven minutes with each of your direct reports or supervisors a day, you will most likely never have any issues. It may be awkward at first, but familiarity brings out the depth of the person and cuts through the surface points. This discussion drives the real meaning of the individual and builds a sense of purpose and insight.

In 2019, I will celebrate my thirty-ninth wedding anniversary with my wife and best friend, Mary Paula. When asked by others what the secret is to a long marriage, I respond this way:

> I believe a good marriage is a 60–40 proposition. Now, before you start sending me hate mail, let me explain. Each of us needs to put 60 percent of ourselves into the marriage and only take out 40 percent. This way, there is always another 40 percent to be taken out by the one who may need it most. In times of sorrow or sickness, good times and bad, there is an extra "bank" of goodwill to be used by the other. We will always have more in the kitty than we take out. Give and take, but mostly give.

For every relationship you have, you need to work daily on it. It is also true for friendships and relationships in business. In today's world of social media, instant messaging, and sending photos in milliseconds across the globe, there is no reason why you can't stay in touch with another human on the planet.

While it is good to keep up with family, friends, and coworkers using Facebook, LinkedIn, Instagram, Twitter, and other programs, there is nothing better than picking up the phone to call, or visit or write a letter. These are the personal touches which are more valuable than gold.

When relationships go sour, saying you are sorry goes a long way. Even if you are right and you want to stand your ground, these two words can and will change the trajectory of the conversation. You need to drop the pride, show some humility, and make this work.

## RELATIONSHIPS ARE LIKE SAVINGS ACCOUNTS

You are building relationships every minute of the day. Every time you have an interaction, you are either making a deposit or taking a withdrawal. It would be best if you found ways to make macro deposits and make micro-loans. You want to have the most substantial balance possible, which keeps growing over time.

One way to do this is to give a nod and a kind word to those who serve you. Always speak to the waiters and waitresses, the cleaning crews, and those behind the counter. They are there to help you, and whom do you think they will help first—the guy who is rude to them or the guy who thanks them? How you treat the waitstaff reveals and is a reflection of your personality and self. What you do and how you project yourself is situational professionalism at its best. It is a character-building exercise wrapped up in daily interactions with those who are working to serve you. A kind word, a small smile, and a handshake make a world of difference and can have a positive effect on them and others who are watching.

When you treat others with respect, it is a reflection of who you are and whom you are becoming. If you want to build your movement and be known for something, this is an excellent place to look. Never underestimate this one leadership trait. Raising the self-worth of others will get you the highest return on your savings account.

### BUSINESSES BUILT ON RELATIONSHIPS

Leadership is all about learning how to get the job done through others, developing effective and awesome teams, reducing friction from their role, and returning the most possible to the organization.

Through creating and nurturing relationships, inside and outside of your business, you bring a full bandwidth of talent and engagement of the teams needed for success.

Relationships are the agent of change to every organization, and you decide the direction they will take. Build yourself. Build up others. Build relationships.

You get more than you give when you give more than you get.

## HIGHLIGHTS OF CHAPTER FIVE

- Personal respect of those you lead
- Show me your friends, and I will show you your future
- Trust is the bedrock of building relationships
- A simple hello
- Become interested in the other person first
- The art of showing up
- No relationship is perfect
- You must work daily on relationships
- Treat relationships like savings accounts
- Businesses built on relationships
- You get more than you give when you give more than you get

## CHAPTER SIX

# COMMUNICATE, COMMUNICATE, COMMUNICATE

*Wise men speak because they have something to say. Fools because they have to say something.*

—PLATO

*We never listen when we are eager to speak.*

—LOUISE VON FRANCOIS

*Be brief. Be bright. Be gone.*

—ANONYMOUS

James Humes, an author, former presidential speechwriter, and one of the writers of the text on the Apollo 11 lunar plaque, said it so well: "The art of communication is the language of leadership."

Notice he uses the word art and not science.

The word art fits better because the world of art is forever changing, moving, evolving. It takes on different forms, textures and mediums, ever-changing based on the creator and their mindset while in the act of creating. The value and skill in a piece of art are highly subjective and do not line up to a set, consistent number of standards. In other words, beauty is in the eye of the beholder.

Science, on the other hand, uses principles, laws, and absolutes. It uses the scientific method of observation, developing a hypothesis, testing, and developing a conclusion. It looks at one single variable, ruling out the influence of other possible variables of the test.

In the end, art is more fluid, while science is like concrete. Art also expresses knowledge in various forms, from the creator's eye while science uses a system to acquire knowledge.

It is this subjectivity on both sides of the equation which causes much of the breakdowns and problems in communication today. How often have we heard or have we said the following statements: "I didn't say that" or "That's not what you said" and "This is what I heard you say."

The most straightforward transaction is when you say something and the receiver hears something different, and at this split second is when the wheels fall off in the conversation. Miscommunication has occurred. The words following miscommunication are always frightening, such as words like a mistake, mishap, and misunderstanding, as well as accident, error, and apologies.

Effective communication is a leadership quality which must continue to be nurtured, practiced, and enhanced. The language of leadership takes on many forms. It can be simple or complex, soft or forceful, and crystal clear or confusing. It is spoken, written, or visual. Body language, voice inflection, and tone introduce another dimension into the conversation as well as the words you choose and the place or time you use them. You decide which variable to add in every interaction.

## EMOTIONAL INTELLIGENCE

Having open, honest, and direct communication is essential for productive and meaningful dialogues. This approach is the first step, with an understanding of one's emotional intelligence.

There are many signs of high emotional intelligence in the workplace. They all center around emotions and how to understand, manage, and display them internally and to others. Ask yourself how you handle your feelings and emotional baggage? To be in touch with yourself will allow you to become more in contact with others on an emotional level.

Learn to take a breath before jumping into conversations. By giving yourself a slight moment before you speak, it will allow you time to assess the situation and respond appropriately. Before speaking, be aware of how others feel, and how to express and control those feelings along with an understanding of how to be empathetic and supportive.

Avoid negative feedback, which can be detrimental to

the feelings of others. Reframe any comments with constructive advice as well as questions, to get their input and give you additional insight into their understanding of the issues. Sincerely provide praise and appreciation whenever possible. Everyone wants to know where one stands, and in providing this feedback, you build a deeper relationship along with trust. The best way to find out if you can trust someone is to believe them.

### COMMUNICATION IS A TWO-WAY PROCESS

You have heard the old saying, "it takes two to tango," and just like dancing, you must have a partner when communicating. It is also a two-way street. While you are trying to talk to them, they are trying to talk to you. It is a give-and-take proposition. Each one is willing to participate in the dance of communication.

Communication happens in an instant. We all do drive-bys, where we lob a sentence or thought at someone as we walk by them or through email, expecting the receiver to know what we want and to make it happen. It is pure insanity at best. While there are some individuals we all "click with" and who can read each other's thoughts, while in reality, they are few and far between.

Each of us can improve our communication style and impact. There are plenty of other books which can get into more depth about this topic, and I encourage you to read, practice, and try different techniques to find what works best for you.

For purposes of this chapter, remember there is always a sender or source of the message, through a channel to the receiver. The receiver interprets the words through their frame of reference. Ideally, the receiver will then provide feedback to the sender as to what was their interpretation of the original words. At this point, the receiver can confirm or provide additional messaging for more clarity. If you can get this far, you are doing well. Much gets lost in the translation, and every receiver is tuned differently.

Something every leader must understand is while their direction or response is simple, others will add to it, believing this is what the leader wants. A simple task can morph into something more significant, like a game of telephone.

The game of telephone is straightforward: you stand ten to twenty people in a line, and the first person whispers a message into the ear of the second person, and each person in turn whispers it to the next person, repeating until it reaches the last person. The last person announces the message they received and compares it with the original signal of the first person. Regardless of the words, it will get garbled with errors and doesn't quite match the first message. The retelling of the story, the anxiousness of the receiver, difficulties in hearing, and sometimes the deliberate changing of the words all take place. The simpler the words or phrase, and the fewer people it must go through, the more it remains true to its original form.

All very simple. What could go wrong, besides everything? Know your audience and who will be receiving your communication. Most people do not listen trying to understand; they hear with the need to reply. Moreover, it all happens in an instant, which can lead to a complete understanding or misunderstanding. Practice active listening skills. It is up to the sender to build in the feedback loops to ensure the cycle is complete.

## LEADERS ENCOURAGE OTHERS TO SPEAK

Communication is the grease of business. It helps to smooth out processes and interaction, providing direction for an organization and helps to present its mission, values, and goals. Communication can also inspire the team, who are doing the work of the business.

Leaders encourage others to speak up and be heard. It doesn't take long for a new employee to learn the job and how work gets completed in your business. The leader must encourage each employee to use their current skills, bring their personality to their position, find ways to improve their job, and be able to influence the future of the company. It is this critical point in an employee's career where they learn to like their job, love their job, or hate their job. The supervisor or manager must allow the conversation to spring forth and have a robust discussion about the goals of the area and how they merge themselves into them. Great ideas surface in open environments. Capturing these moments and following through leads to extraordinary accomplishments.

You see it all the time. It takes between three and six months for someone to decide if they are a good fit for an organization and vice versa. The daily and weekly interaction during this time is critical to how employees perceive themselves, their productivity, and cultural fit. Most employees, including yourself, don't wake up in the morning thinking, "I wonder how I can mess things up today?" Instead, based on thousands of conversations I have had with new employees, they are thinking just the opposite—"How can I make an impact in my job, what will I learn today, and what will today bring?" When strong interactions and active communication occurs frequently, the workforce becomes more committed and is willing to go the extra mile for the leader and the organization.

## LISTENING BUILDS TRUST

True leaders open conversations, listen intently, and

respond accordingly. Listening is an underrated skill and one which must be honed and practiced. Are you hearing something different than what is being said? Is there something else the employee is not saying which you are picking up on? Listening builds trust. By listening to understand a point of view or situation, and asking clarification questions with the sender, you develop a mutual sense of confidence which expands over time.

Once you achieve a certain trust level, more ideas and suggestions will flow. It is a turning point in everyone's leadership journey, where employees have better ideas than you have. If you have built mutual trust, then you must be willing to give the employee some latitude with their views. They should own the outcome, and you will hold the follow-up. When you give the green light for them to move forward on their plan, they have a stronger purpose of seeing it through and of being successful. Delegating can be a way for you to do more as a leader than you ever have before.

### DELEGATING

I would be remiss if I didn't spend some time discussing delegation while we discuss effective communication. Empowering your colleagues and other employees is another skillset of a broad leader, which can have a "ten times" impact on the organization. In short, delegating builds trust between you and the employee, and you must know their abilities and capabilities before proceeding. You must be assertive in setting clear goals and expectations. Communication is still at the heart of delegating. The clarity in the expected outcome, the level of authority you are delegating, and allowing for questions and feedback are paramount. As a leader, you must be willing to let go of the task and not micromanage. You will be monitoring the progress and provide any input and training needed. You will stay involved, but from afar. Leadership is all about getting your work done through others.

## MANAGEMENT BY WALKING OR WANDERING AROUND

Part of being a leader is being visible to your employees at every level in the organization. Some great leaders can manage the organization from behind their desk—most can't. Instead of operating by email, I am encouraging you to get up out of your chair and walk to the other person's office. It is OK to sit down and have a conversation with them. You can always follow up with an email, but you are building relationships and putting a face behind your position. Employees want to have face-to-face conversations with the person running the company, department, or region, and by wandering around, you can make yourself more available to your team.

The emphasis is on the word *wandering*. The point is to

be unstructured and meeting with employees outside of customarily scheduled meetings. The leader gets a better understanding of the current work throughout their departments and provides the employee with a way to ask questions on a project, get additional direction, and give direct updates. These random encounters can provide a sense of importance and purpose, which can lead to more job satisfaction and productivity.

Don't underestimate the importance of spontaneous visits and being seen walking the halls and showing up. Abraham Lincoln was a fan of this management style. He informally would ride out to inspect the Union troops during the American Civil War. The benefits were numerous.

## TWO EARS AND ONE MOUTH

I will close this chapter with one of my favorite quotes:

> We have two ears and one mouth—listen twice as much as you speak.

The attributed quote is from a Greek philosopher, Epictetus, born in the first century, who believed that individuals are responsible for their actions and must examine and control through constant, rigorous self-discipline. He thought external events were outside of one's control and we should accept them calmly and dispassionately. He also maintained an individual's foundation is self-knowledge and to expose yourself to as many situations as practical, to learn and decipher a proper course. He also lived by strong convictions of ethics and distinguishing things within our power and those not in our control.

If you can open your ears, then you can open your mind. We learn by touch, observation, reading, and listening. If you are speaking, then you are repeating what you already know. By allowing others to talk, it grants insight as to how they think and what they consider important and essential. You will learn much more when you listen twice as much as you speak.

## HIGHLIGHTS OF CHAPTER SIX

- The art of communication is the language of leadership
- Emotional intelligence
- Communication is a two-way process
- The game of telephone
- Leaders encourage others to speak
- Communication is the grease of business
- Listening builds trust
- Delegating
- Management by wandering around
- Two ears and one mouth—listen twice as much as you speak

## CHAPTER SEVEN

# IDEAS, INNOVATION, AND PLANNING

*A pile of rocks ceases to be a rock when somebody contemplates it with the idea of a cathedral in mind.*

—ANTOINE DE SAINT-EXUPÉRY

*Vision is the art of seeing the invisible.*

—JONATHAN SWIFT

*If you fail to plan, you are planning to fail.*

—BENJAMIN FRANKLIN

In 1899, just as the turn of the century was coming of age, Charles Holland Duell, the Commissioner of the US Patent Office was misquoted. This statement was incorrectly attributed to him, stating, "Everything that can be invented, has been invented." His vision was quite the opposite, stating, "I almost wish that I might live my life over again to see the wonders which are at the threshold."

Mr. Duell would have been quite pleased with all the wonders of the twenty-first century.

It happens all the time. Change is constant. Ideas are flowing; humanity continues to shape their environment, landscape, and world.

The world thrives on information and ideas. New, old, recycled—it doesn't matter. We are always in constant motion, looking for the next great thing. Concepts have no limit; they start with problems to fix, imagination as big as the universe and beyond, as well as dreams of what could be. It may take the stacking of ideas or the combination of various thoughts, which molds into a thing of beauty.

There are no perfect ideas or silver bullets, but rather flashes of light and brilliance, which captures the essence and meaning with vivid color.

The "wonders which are at the threshold," are still yet

to be. You are part of the grand process to bring these wonders to the surface and bring them to life.

Moreover, it starts with your knowledge and ideas, your frame of reference and experience, and your creativity and innovation.

The only thing holding you back are the limits you place on yourself. You now have permission to open and expand your mind and experiences and push your personal and professional boundaries. Once broadened, you will rarely go back to your original shape and are changed forever.

## IDEAS

We all have ideas, imaginations, and dreams. Humans are a creative force in this universe, hoping for a better life, a better place, and a better world.

We need to take time to daydream and think, and ask if there is a better way to do things while dreaming about the possibilities of change and innovation. What information is available to us, how can we get more, and is it quantity over quality or a balance of both?

Ideas are just ideas—neither good nor bad in your sandbox. They are ideas of your mind. It would be best if you released them and put them on paper or typed them into a document. Then you could begin to visualize them, touch them, and mold them. There is no one way to do anything! There are many paths to an outcome. Keep your mind open to other trails to follow.

You need to be able to question your ideas with boldness. Why does it have to be this way? Is there a better way to do this? "We have always done it this way" doesn't hold water any longer. Times have changed, and maybe the time wasn't right for the idea when presented, but now it is.

Think of when Henry Ford imagined, innovated, and created the first mass-produced automobile. He famously said, "Any customer can have a car painted any color that he wants so long as it is black." His statement is just the start of a new idea. Why do cars have to be black?

In Mr. Ford's world, in the early twentieth century, black was the only color paint that could dry quickly. He created the first production line and needed all the parts to be ready as soon as possible so the line would not slow down. The technology was in its infancy, and they didn't have the chemistry or chemicals developed to make fast-drying paint happen.

Fast forward to now—you can get any automobile painted any color or colors your heart desires. Progress on so many fronts have changed the ways autos are built, shaped, and sold. Changes keep being made because the next generation of car owners and engineers are asking more "what if" questions.

Another hard fact and truth—there are more ideas than time to do them all. Everyone has thoughts and ideas—and good ones too. The reality of only having twenty-four hours in a day is that you can't do them all. You must nurture good ideas, challenge others, and begin to prioritize those with promise. Others you need to stop working on as their time may not be now. It would be best if you continued to learn how and when to say no or not right now.

Brainstorming is a beautiful way to get ideas out in the open by harnessing everyone's creativity and thoughts. No idea is a bad idea. You need to capture each one because it may play a role in triggering other viewpoints that could enhance a good idea and make it even better.

Necessity is the most significant idea generator around. The "mother of invention" lies in problems and those who believe they can build a better mousetrap. Problem-solving is a very human trait learned by trial and error, or sheer determination to improve on prior inventions.

If you get inquisitive, go to the US Patent and Trademark Office and look up how many inventions there are for mousetraps. By the last count, the patent office has issued over 4,400 mousetrap patents. Guess how many of them have made any money? Only about two dozen or so. Most of them work to some degree but working and being commercially viable are two very different things.

Ideation is at the beginning of this process. Let the ideas flow.

## THINK BIG

While interviewing for an executive position, the psychologist conducting the interview wanted to see the scope and breadth of my ability to generate lines of thought while under pressure. I called this exercise the "explosion of thought."

The instructions were relatively straightforward. I was to generate as many implications as possible during a fifteen-minute exercise, answering one question. The question was:

> Scientists have just created a pill, which is mass-produced for pennies, has no harmful human effects—no matter how many are consumed—and provides the individual with enough nourishment and sustenance for a day. What are the implications?

The clock starts now. Go.

My mind started racing with ideas.

I immediately wrote in bullet points:

- World hunger solved
- World population increases
- The agricultural industry in peril
- Loss of jobs in food service, heavy farm equipment and more
- Nations with agrarian economies collapse
- Political balance changes in countries
- Society weakens—less social time eating together
- The arts and entertainment take off due to extra time
- Health issues solved—obesity, diabetes, fewer heart attacks, and now hospitals are not relevant

Each time I wrote an idea, it generated another line of thought. These mini explosions sent pathways like lightning, breaking off into other areas of consciousness. It was like Alice falling down the rabbit hole, a journey which was complicated and chaotic as different paths developed with the next thought. I couldn't write fast enough, and when finished with an idea, I went back to another fork in the road, tripping down, and developed more implications on implications.

I did reasonably well after receiving the results. The personal pathways of thought which you develop, which come from your frame of reference and experiences, show how broad and thick they are. How you conceptualize your place in the world—locally, regionally, nationally and worldly—provide a glimpse of how you solve problems, look for resources, and imagine and organize your mind.

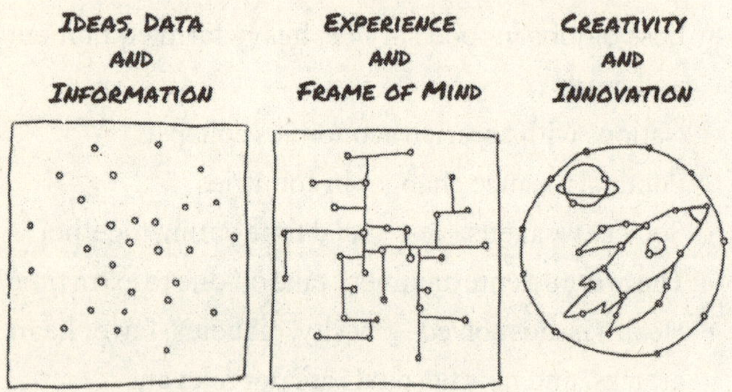


Jakob Klar, Illustrator

The dots are the same in each frame.

How do you look at the world and connect the dots you see?

This explosion of thought then lays a framework for aligning concepts and connecting them, which results in a structure of action—innovation.

## INNOVATION

Ideas are beautiful, but at the end of the day, they are still concepts. Ideas are just dreams without wings. They require little action on the dreamer's part. It is all about putting the pieces together and bringing it to life.

The difference between creativity and innovation is as big as night and day. Being creative is all about stretching the mind, being open to new possibilities, and seeing the same thing but thinking of something different. Innovation is about doing new things.

In the early 1970s, Martin Cooper was asked to design the first car phone for Motorola, the predecessor of our current cell phones. They used radio technology to connect the handset to a base unit, to link to the copper wires of the telephone system. They were creating ideas and building on previous knowledge, changing the current system to unlock new value and opportunities.

Mr. Cooper and his team didn't just jump in with the idea of a phone in a car. They asked questions about the current state of phone service in the world, the problems they were trying to solve, and other possible applications. They came up with a simple question: when you wanted to call someone, why did you have to call a specific place? You had to call their home or work, or wherever you believed they might be.

This idea and questioning was the pivot to a new line of thinking. Why do we call places instead of people?

You need to develop a curious mind. Be curious about the world, how things work, and about people. Doing things the same way they have always been done before doesn't lead to success. It is those who remain curious who are the dreamers, distant in thought and able to ask the questions others are not willing to ask.

In 2002, Elon Musk asked, "Why can't we reduce the cost of space travel by reusing the rockets after launch?" His question disrupted the aerospace industry with his firm SpaceX.

"Why do we have to stay in hotels while traveling, focusing on experiences rather than possessions?" asked Brian Chesky, as he created an online marketplace for home-sharing, starting a company called Airbnb in 2008.

"Why do we have to ride in a taxi?" Garrett Camp asked in 2009, as he spent hundreds of dollars on a private driver, looking for ways to reduce the expense of black car services. So, he founded Uber.

"How can we reduce the cost of transactions in the cryptocurrency space, allowing merchants and consumers to complete transactions using new digital currencies?"

asked Fred Ehrsam, a former Goldman Sachs trader, and Brian Armstrong, a past engineer at Airbnb, as they established Coinbase in 2012. This platform is a win-win for merchants, because the fees are less than what they pay to process credit card transactions, and for consumers, it opens this up to the masses at a lower cost.

How many more opportunities are there to be creative and disruptive? Remember the words of Mr. Charles Holland Duell waiting to "see all of the wonders which are at the threshold."

## PLANNING

The next logical step in this process, after idea generation and innovation, is the planning phase and adding wings to the ideas.

Leaders set their priorities and ways to get things done. The art of planning is as old as time and done instinctively. You are continually making small, minute plans every second of your day. You are shifting through various options each second, making minor corrections to your plan.

PLAN AHEAD

Here is a way to illustrate this concept. If you are driving to work, you have a plan. Moreover, this plan needs constant course changes to get you to your goal. Once you turn your key in the ignition, the car needs input from you as to what to do next. You have been trained to follow a "plan" to get the car into motion. Then, while driving to work, you are turning the wheel, ever so slightly, to keep the vehicle in its lane, stopping when appropriate and maneuvering into a parking spot.

You received thousands of inputs which needed decisions, sorting, and action. Items such as weather, road conditions, and traffic were taken into consideration to get you to your goal. All you did was execute the plan which you have done hundreds of times. Your experience was vital in this planning, evaluating, and execution.

Much like in the idea phase, there is always an abundance of options. The options available to you are more numerous than the stars. The objective is your guiding light—any must do's, limits, or restrictions specified.

There is no right or wrong time limit for planning. It depends on how minor or critical the objective is. If the decision can't wait until tomorrow, then you need information today. If you are planning next year's vacation, then you have time to gather options. If there are competitive pressures, then the action is needed sooner than later. You also don't want to be caught in "analysis paralysis" where you are overloaded with information, details, and numbers where you can't make a decision. Most successful leaders tend to err on the side of action, rather than inaction.

Planning always begins by asking the right questions. The opposite is a real danger as well—wasting time and energy, answering the wrong questions. An easy way to remember this is an old British military adage called the Five Ps of Success:

## PROPER PREPARATION PREVENTS POOR PERFORMANCE

Planning is a skill to master if you want to get more done. Keeping the end in mind will assist you in determining what your plan tends to become.

There are many tools available to give you an assist with project management and large projects. The focus now will be much narrower, concentrating on what you can do at the moment. Action planning can be distilled down to a simple logic diagram with the following statement:

*If this, then that.*

IFTTT is a conditional statement chain which helps to automate decisions with predetermined outcomes. The human brain can calculate thousands of these statements in a flash, based on prior learnings, knowledge, and experiences.

Returning to our car example, an easy IFTTT is: if day turns to night, then turn on headlights. If it is raining, then turn on windshield wipers.

The statement requires an action. If something expected or not expected occurs, and the condition is met, then a predetermined operation will follow. The more you can determine the next steps, the more IFTTT statements you can chain, automating the outcome with consistency and speed.

A hallmark of leadership is the exhibited behaviors of planning and executing. By developing the concepts of ideation, innovation, along with creating a solid plan, the leader will continue to produce and establish a well-structured team ready to take on anything.

## HIGHLIGHTS OF CHAPTER SEVEN

- Change is constant
- Necessity is the most significant idea generator
- Take ideas through an "explosion of thought"
- Ideas are just dreams without wings
- Innovation is about doing new things
- You need to develop a curious mind
- Planning always begins by asking the right question
- Proper Planning Prevents Poor Performance
- If this, then that
- Do your homework

# CHAPTER EIGHT

# DISCIPLINE AND FOCUS

*Discipline is choosing between what you want now and what you want most.*

—ABRAHAM LINCOLN

*If you chase two rabbits, both will escape.*

—AUTHOR UNKNOWN

86,400 seconds.

1,440 minutes.

24 hours.

One day.

Time never stops. It is the great equalizer. You can't bank time or gather it up for later. Once it is gone, it is gone. You can try to save time by cutting corners, multitasking or skipping steps, but in the end, how did that work out for you? What about getting more efficient at a task, learning new skills, or developing yourself through reading, education, or being present in the moment?

Tick tock.

Time continues to slip through the hourglass whether you are rich or poor, young or old, starting your career or family, or getting ready to retire.

Every person in the world gets the same amount of time as everyone else. Every day, you get a new opportunity for how you are going to spend your time. Maybe the better question is, how are you going to invest your time? What investments will you make in yourself today to be better tomorrow?

We all typically start off the day the same—we lay in bed as our eyes slowly open and focus on the clock or phone. However, after that, it's all about choice. Are you going to get right up, or roll over? Are you going to pick up your phone and look at messages or emails, or do you have someplace to be? Are you starting your day off ahead of schedule, or will you be "behind the clock" all day? How you spend your time is your choice.

Tick tock.

Sure, it is easy to fill up your day with things to do, shows to watch, classes or meetings to attend. Many of you have responsibilities for others, but in the end, it is your time.

If you do not plan your time, your time will plan you. If you don't give a block of time a name and make a commitment at that time, you cannot get back lost time. You will have to try to fit it in your day and move other priorities to make it work.

However, who are you making it work for, yourself or others? As a leader, it is even more important to think of how you are using your time because it just does not affect you—it affects everyone who works for you and even your company.

There are always time thieves throughout the day, so it is

essential to be on constant guard. Time thieves can often come to you in disguise. A friend or colleague comes to you for help with a problem or situation and suddenly, someone else's problem becomes yours. Don't let them leave their monkey on your desk. Have the courage to ask how they are going to fix it and let them handle it. Not my monkey, not my circus.

Tick tock.

Think of time as a commodity, a valuable resource slipping through your fingers if not given the proper care and attention. Time is your time, and something everyone wants to take. You decide to share it with others. You choose where you spend it, what you do with it and when to give it away. You can use it wisely or foolishly—it is yours to give freely or to hold tightly.

If you want to get more out of your time, have the sense of accomplishment and find the time you never thought you had before, this chapter is an investment in your future you can use every day.

## DISCIPLINE AND FOCUS

You always start at the beginning, and in this case, it is with yourself. You are the only one who can make the change. You must be the change within you.

Everyone has faults. My guess is you know yours all too well. These are the little things that drive us crazy—we live with them daily, and we are not willing to share them with others.

The question is, "When will you change?" No one shouts from the mountaintops the things we hide inside. To change something, you first must acknowledge it and accept the current state.

Are you five, ten, or twenty pounds overweight? Do you bite your nails? Are you a poor speller? Are you always late for meetings? Do you have a messy desk or bedroom, or kitchen?

If you want to be skinny, then do the things that thin people do. If you're going to stop biting your nails, then stop biting your nails. Are you a poor speller? There is no reason in the world today to not be a good speller! Use the tools, the autocorrect, and your phone for goodness sakes!

It takes discipline on your part and a focus to become better every day. Sounds too simple, but you need your commitment to change and to do that change over and over.

Discipline can be either action or inaction. You can either

decide to go to the gym every day or have the control to avoid desserts in the evening. You must be willing to change your behavior.

Doing those behaviors and things you currently are doing have gotten you to this point. How's that working for you? If you always do what you have always done, you will always get what you've always got. Once you change your behaviors and do something different, you will get a different result.

Focus goes hand in hand with discipline. The ability to focus is the art of concentrating and keeping the interest or activity right in front of you. You can adjust the focus on a camera, so the object you are viewing is sharp and clear. Your goal needs to be like a laser beam, and then have the discipline to move closer and faster to your goal.

Many times we know what we need to do, but we don't want to do it. When paralyzed with doubt, do. You must set aside the time—give the task a name and a time frame, and then start. How often have you put off starting a job and then when you did it, it wasn't as bad as you thought, or it didn't take as much time as you had planned? Often. The key is starting.

It happens most when you focus on the obstacle rather than the outcome. You might tell yourself, "I don't know how to start" or "What do I do first?" First things first—start with the end in mind, what you want to accomplish and then begin. What is the job to be done? Do anything to start.

Are you a painter or a sculptor? A painter thinks additively while a sculptor thinks reductively. The painter starts with nothing and applies layers of paint, while the sculptor begins with something and removes parts of it.

It is like the sculptor who was chipping away at a piece of marble, creating an elephant. A student asked him, "How do you know what to chip away?" The artist replied, "I just chip away everything that doesn't look like an elephant." Just get in there and start doing something, and a path will reveal itself to you. Steve Jobs once said, "You can't connect the dots looking forward; you can only connect them looking backward. So, you have to trust that the dots will somehow connect in your future."

Many times you do not want to start—or finish—something because you may make a mistake. This fear is understandable but must be overcome to reach your goal. Mistakes can be fixed if they are not fatal. Errors are the price of learning. Without them, we would not have beautiful pieces of art, remarkable writings, and cultural progress. Wear your failures as a badge of honor. I would rather have my teams trying new ideas and programs and failing, then have them stay with the tried-and-true. Thomas Edison said, "I have not failed. I have just found 10,000 ways that won't work."

You get results by focusing on the actions that produce results. You need to break down a task into bite-size pieces, so you can have a sense of accomplishment and drive to do more. If you lament on cutting the grass every week, make a game out of it. Break up your yard into various squares and then cut the squares at random. Time yourself on how fast you can mow and set a goal to beat your time. Don't just mow up and down. Change it. Make the task exciting but keep focused on the purpose of cutting your lawn and the discipline to do it weekly.

Focus is more important than intelligence. Being focused is a complicated thing to do as there are always distractions at every turn. It is those employees who can get something accomplished, finish the task and ready to take on more, which will be the new capital of the future—the critical component to getting more from life, enjoying life and having more time for life. To be purpose-driven, achieving results, and doing it with a smile, will make you valuable beyond belief.

I want to share another story with you called "Take Action Sooner than Later." It highlights another dimension of discipline and focus, which calls for getting things done on time or sooner.

### TAKE ACTION SOONER THAN LATER

"You owe me a one-hundred-dollar bill," said August Busch III, CEO of Anheuser-Busch Companies during a lunch meeting with me in Tampa, Florida. "You can bring it to me next weekend."

He stood up from the table and walked back to his helicopter with the group and left.

"Does he really want me to bring him a hundred-dollar bill?" I said to the group.

"If I were you, I would!" was almost the unanimous reply.

Let me rewind and take it from the beginning.

I proudly worked for Anheuser-Busch for thirteen-plus years as the vice president of human resources and training at Busch Gardens in Tampa, Florida. Growing up in St. Louis, Missouri, it was the dream of most, including me, to someday work for A-B. They were the largest, most well-respected, and admired company in America, and they were local. They had strong values and supported a multitude of community and national charities. Quality was at the top of the list—quality of products, service, and employees.

I am also a big fan and admirer of August Busch III. Being able to work for an industry titan and learn from him was the equivalent of a master's degree. Walking the park with him and watching what was important to him—providing the best care to the animal collection, quality, stunning visuals and memorable experiences for the guests, and solid financials for his theme parks—created a sense of ownership and pride in making the parks leaders in the industry.

Mr. Busch would winter in Florida and make frequent visits to Busch Gardens in Tampa and SeaWorld in Orlando. It would not be uncommon to see him and others from St. Louis in the parks, on the weekends, twenty to thirty times a year.

As part of the executive team, we would be at the park on the weekends to meet him, tour the park and have a lunch meeting. He gave us insight into the direction of the company, the beer industry, financials, and competitor updates with the team. It was common for him to ask each person at the table questions about their departments and follow-ups from previous visits. He had a keen memory for details, numbers, and people.

During one lunch meeting, it seemed like everyone was getting questions about their departments, their numbers, and the industry. After Mr. Busch left, we gathered in an office, and everyone compared notes and helped each other determine what follow-ups were needed. There was also a group of executives waiting in St. Louis to help us gather the beer industry reports and anything else we needed. They typically asked, "What does chief want this week?" and they would work over the weekend and get us what we needed for the following weekend's visit.

Unfortunately for me, the next weekend arrived without a few reports on the 401(k) and pension plans.

Mr. Busch arrived on time where the team met him and started our tour of the park. During the walk, he would ask for various vice presidents to walk with him and provide him with updates. We arrived for lunch and continued answering his questions. He asked for me and I took the seat to his right and started to show him various reports. He asked for the 401(k) reports for the company, and I told him they were not ready, but I would have them next week.

It felt like time stopped. Mr. Busch slowly put down his fork and slid his back against the chair while grasping his hands. He turned to me and said to me, "You do not have the 401(k) numbers I asked for last week?"

"No, sir, I don't," I replied.

Mr. Busch took a deep breath. "Do you have the pension reports for those employees with thirty and thirty-five years as I asked for last week?" he said as he closed his eyes and dropped his head.

"No, sir. I will have them this weekend," I said as I winced slightly.

He raised his head and looked at me and said sternly, "You lost the bet. You owe me a hundred bucks."

"Pardon me?" I said softly.

"You heard me. You lost the bet, and when I return next week, I expect you to bring a hundred-dollar bill and the reports you didn't bring this week." At that point, he stood up, pushed away from the table, and headed to the helicopter. Everyone else stood up and joined him on his walk back. I lagged behind the others as he left the property.

This was not good.

The group all convened in an office to review next week's requests. The mood was very heavy. I let down my team, my president, and myself.

That next week, I doubled and tripled my attention and focus on the task at hand. It was my responsibility to get these reports, make sure they were accurate, and have them ready when Mr. Busch stepped off the helicopter. I was on the phone with those who had the data, produced the slides, and could help me interpret and provide insight into the numbers. I prepared like I never had in the past.

It was a very long week.

By the time the weekend arrived, I had rehearsed, challenged, and knew these numbers inside and out. I even prepared a deck for questions that he asked in the past, but hadn't in the last several visits.

The team was waiting near the field looking through their notes, talking on their phones and to each other.

I don't know if you ever get used to hearing the rotors of a helicopter when you are anticipating a visit. The pulsating sound with a distinctive chop, chop, chop reminds me of the opening of M.A.S.H. That is what it felt like to me this day.

The helicopter landed. Mr. Busch stepped out. He looked around the field and then he saw me. He raised his forearm and motioned with his index finger to come over.

I started walking towards him, ducking my head and shoulders as the rotors slowed.

"Do you have something for me?" he said while still turning his head, looking over the field.

I reached into my pocket and pulled out a crisp one-hundred-dollar bill that I had gotten from the credit union mid-week and presented it to him.

He looked at the bill, took it with his right hand, and grabbed the other side, tugging at the bill several times. He slightly smiled as he put the money in his shirt pocket and walked past me towards the group. I did all I could to catch up, and was never called to walk with him through the park.

We arrived for lunch, and the last seat was the one farthest away. Mr. Busch started to ask for his updates, and one by one, the vice presidents answered. The mood at the table was lively, engaging, and informative. There was laughter with great discussion. Mr. Busch made a motion that it was my turn in the seat. I was the last to be called.

I sat next to him, and he looked around the table as he asked me, "Gary, do you have any updates for me?"

"Yes, I do, Mr. Busch." I showed him the 401(k) graphs and discussed participation rates, calculations of the 401(k) contribution rates over the past five years, differences between divisions, age groups, and investment selections. We had a perfect dialogue on the pension program, talking through the current vesting schedules, what long-term employees would receive when they retired, and communication programs. I even had other charts and data comparing the industry retirement programs.

I was fully prepared. I answered every question Mr. Busch threw out and then some. I was concise, knowledgeable, and ready to carry on more deliberation on the topic. Also, I had no follow-ups for next week. At least, that's what I thought.

He then looked over at me and said, "Do you have a pen?"

A pen? Now he wants my pen, I thought with a puzzled look. "Yes sir, I do," I said and handed him my pen.

He looked at the pen, pulled the hundred-dollar bill from his front pocket, and wrote, "Take action sooner than later. August."

"This is a lesson for you. I am running a multibillion-dollar industry in an ever-changing environment. We need to be fast, agile, and able to make decisions quickly. When I ask for something, I expect it to be a priority. I do not have the luxury of time to wait for you or anyone else. I need data to make decisions. I wrote, 'Take action sooner than later,' and you need to remember and keep this front of mind and act accordingly."

"I understand, and it won't happen again," I replied.

"Good," he said as he handed me the pen and the hundred-dollar bill. "I will be here next week. I want you to have this prominently displayed in your office, and I will look next time I am in town."

One more follow-up.

He stood up, pushed himself back from the table, congratulated the team on a job well done, and headed back to the helicopter.

True to his word, the next week upon landing at the park, first thing off the helicopter, he grabbed a golf cart, motioned for me to get in and drove to my office where he saw the hundred-dollar bill displayed on my credenza.

He smiled slightly and said, "Good. Let's go walk the park."

"Sooner than later" has become my battle cry, a reminder that when you are in a position of leadership and people depend on you, you don't want to let them down.

## HIGHLIGHTS OF CHAPTER EIGHT

- Time is the great equalizer
- Time is a commodity, your valuable resource
- Identify your faults and commit to change
- Discipline can be either action or inaction
- Focus is the art of concentrating, keeping your goal in front of you
- Focus on the outcome rather than the obstacle
- Mistakes can be fixed, as long as they are not fatal
- Focus on actions that produce results
- Focus is more important than intelligence
- Sooner than later—get tasks done on time at any cost

# BONUS CHAPTER I

## BREAK IT DOWN—3X3X3

*Do the difficult things while they are easy and do the great things when they are small. A journey of a thousand steps begins with a single step.*

—LAO TZU

*A short pencil is better than a long memory.*

—GARY VIEN

*Do it today, so you don't have to tomorrow.*

—SOME UNKNOWN POOR SOUL WHO GOT IN TROUBLE

Let's dive right in.

You want to get things done.

You don't know where to start, but you have an idea of what you want.

It's time to stop the procrastination and let me show you a method to get things done.

## BREAK IT DOWN

You can do anything! All you need to do is break down any goal into bite-size tasks and start doing them, then check them off your list.

I am not going to teach you anything you don't know already. All I am going to do is give you a tool and a framework to get down on paper the essence of the steps towards your goal, for you to get there faster, make a more significant impact, or be able to get on to the next big thing.

You will be able to do this anywhere and anytime by breaking a task down to only three key elements. Then you will further define those three goals into smaller goals. After you get to nine smaller jobs, you can break them down even more by breaking those goals into three each, giving you an additional twenty-seven tasks to complete.

Let me break it down as to how you can apply this to your routine.

Ever need to speak to a group or make a ten-minute presentation? Here is an ideal solution to write your speech.

Let's go through a sample of what you can do. Start with a topic you want to talk on, such as buying a car. Break the subtopics into three sections you want to discuss. For example:

GOAL: BUYING A CAR

- Preparing to buy a car
- Purchasing a car
- Maintenance of your car

Then you can break those three sections into three more parts with further topics for your presentation, such as:

SMART GOAL: BUY A CAR FOR UNDER $20,000 WITHIN THREE MONTHS

- Preparing to buy a car
  - Determining a budget
  - Type of car
  - Financing for my vehicle
- Purchasing a vehicle

    - Selecting a dealership
    - Test driving
    - Negotiating the deal
- Maintenance of your vehicle
    - Insurance
    - Read the owner's manual
    - Scheduled maintenance

Now that you have this detail, do you think you could give a ten-minute talk with a goal, three sections, and sub-sections? Can you talk for one minute on each of these?

I am sure you can!

## HOW TO USE THE 3X3X3 METHOD

1. Define what goal you want to accomplish. Best to make it a SMART goal—Specific, Measurable, Attainable, Relevant, and Time-Based. Write this at the top of the page.
2. Break down this goal into three essential tasks and write them below the goal.
3. Further, break down these three critical tasks into three smaller tasks and write them below the appropriate key task. This now gives you nine sub or secondary jobs.
4. If needed, you can further define these nine secondary tasks into an additional twenty-seven tasks.

Use this format by using bullet points:

START WITH YOUR SMART GOAL

1. Key Task
   - Sub-Task
   - Sub-Task
   - Sub-Task

2. Key Task
   - Sub-Task
   - Sub-Task
   - Sub-Task

3. Key Task
   - Sub-Task
   - Sub-Task
   - Sub-Task

If you need more detail or want to break it down into mouth-size tasks to give specific direction, break it down to the next level.

For illustration, let's show you only the first critical key task.

WRITE YOUR SMART GOAL HERE

1. Key Task
   - A. Sub-Task
     - I. Secondary Task
     - II. Secondary Task
     - III. Secondary Task
   - B. Sub-Task
     - I. Secondary Task
     - II. Secondary Task
     - III. Secondary Task
   - C. Sub-Task
     - I. Secondary Task
     - II. Secondary Task
     - III. Secondary Task

Some like to put the sub-tasks on the top of the page and run each of the sub and secondary tasks down the page in swim lanes, such as in the following illustration:

WRITE YOUR SMART GOAL HERE

| 1. KEY TASK | 2. KEY TASK | 3. KEY TASK |
|---|---|---|
| A. Sub-Task | A. Sub-Task | A. Sub-Task |
| i. | i. | i. |
| ii. | ii. | ii. |
| iii. | iii. | iii. |
| B. Sub-Task | B. Sub-Task | B. Sub-Task |
| i. | i. | i. |
| ii. | ii. | ii. |
| iii. | iii. | iii. |
| C. Sub-Task | C. Sub-Task | C. Sub-Task |
| i. | i. | i. |
| ii. | ii. | ii. |
| iii. | iii. | iii. |

Break your goals down, think in threes, and start checking items off your to-do list!

# BONUS CHAPTER II

## WISDOM FOR FUTURE LEADERS

*Is there anyone so wise as to learn by the experience of others?*

—VOLTAIRE

*From the errors of others, a wise man corrects his own.*

—PUBLILIUS SYRUS

*A leader is a dealer in hope.*

—NAPOLEON BONAPARTE

I have met and worked with many extraordinary leaders throughout my career while working and traveling around the world. Some of them you have heard of through stories in this book, while the others have made their mark on my development through direct supervision, observation, and mentoring. Whether it was my first assistant manager or many bosses, numerous business and community leaders, or those I have served with on various charitable or community boards, they have all had a small part in expanding my frame of reference in developing my style of leadership and contributed to my success.

While all are thought leaders in their industry and business sectors, they are also regular people who care deeply about their causes, their families, their communities, and leaving something better for future generations. I value their opinions and am proud to call them my friends.

While working on this book, I reached out to many of them for some perspective and guiding words to add another level thought for my readers.

The question I asked was:

**"If you were to speak to the next generation of leaders and could pass along in just a few sentences, the most powerful leadership lesson you gained throughout your career, what would you say to them?"**

I knew they would come through and they did! They offered a variety of insightful and practical advice that you can use throughout your career. Learn from their voices of experience about leadership and what they found invaluable looking back over their career:

*Don't be afraid to let others make mistakes. If an employee has an idea that they are passionate about, do everything you can to let them try it, even if you have some reservations about it. Consider the downside if it's not successful and, if they're not overly harsh, back your employee. There's probably a good chance of success and, if not, remember what Yoda said in The Last Jedi, "The Best Education, failure it is!*

TOM DORETY, RETIRED CEO, SUNCOAST CREDIT UNION

*Don't over-complicate the processes to meet your objectives. Keep things as simple as possible. Employees will appreciate it. No need to try and impress people by complicating things. It is important to show appreciation to the people who help you reach your objectives. Taking credit for other people's work won't win you any respect.*

MIKE GLENNAN, SENIOR VICE PRESIDENT,
SIX FLAGS CORPORATION, FLUME FOREMAN
& CASUAL POOL HOST (RETIRED)

*Lead from your heart. Be real. Be compassionate. Of course, strategic planning, financial accountability, revenue management, compliance, creative sales, and marketing are all immensely valuable. If you genuinely care about your team members, earnestly listen to them and invite their input, celebrate their accomplishments and allow them to blossom, your business success will resemble that of an Olympic team.*

*Win or lose, you and your entire team will pull together, give their all, and fight to the end for you and each other. Extra time and effort are required, but the rewards can be both financially and emotionally rewarding.*

ROBIN DAVIS CARSON, RETIRED FORMER BUSCH ENTERTAINMENT CORPORATION EXECUTIVE

*Don't take failure as a stop sign. Take each day as an opportunity to become better. Learn from mistakes. Be self-aware. Become the best version of yourself.*

ANDREW DUNCAN, CO-FOUNDER/CEO, FORTIS TECHNOLOGY SOLUTIONS, L.L.C.

*A successful, vibrant organization depends on inspired leadership. A strong leader infuses the organization with a vision and strategy for growth that responds to a changing environment. Further, an effective leader empowers the organization through collaboration, building the capacity of others to assume leadership, being accountable, and promoting a positive work culture. Exemplary leaders instill trust with their actions and consistency—they do the right things for the organization.*

EARL WHITLOCK, ED. D., ADJUNCT PROFESSOR, USF—DEPARTMENT OF EDUCATIONAL LEADERSHIP, AND POLICY STUDIES, RETIRED—HILLSBOROUGH COUNTY PUBLIC SCHOOLS, SCHOOL AND DISTRICT ADMINISTRATOR

*Hard work trumps skill almost every day—don't be afraid to do more. Work harder than anyone else. It will pay off. Be persistent—good ideas are about timing. Don't judge. Keep an eye out for management lessons everywhere. Ask more questions than you give answers. Questions are the best tool we have, so use them often.*

WILLIAM (BILL) W. MOORE, PRESIDENT AND CEO,
ZOO MIAMI FOUNDATION, IMMEDIATE PAST CEO,
KENNEDY SPACE CENTER VISITOR COMPLEX

*To future leaders—continuously grow your network. Expose yourself to different styles of leaders throughout different organizations and even different industries. You may even pick a mentor or two and pick their brain and a lot of "Why?" questions to learn different approaches to solving business challenges and seek out opportunities.*

*Make a quilt of yourself. It starts with you and your beliefs and values, blending in the traits and styles of others which fit your personality or suit your strengths. It is an evolution, and you never stop adapting to those around you, and over time, you will find your most effective leadership style for you and your teams.*

KEVIN D. JOHNSON, PRESIDENT/ CEO, SUNCOAST CREDIT UNION

*Care. Just care. Care about employees as people and individuals, not as employees. Make a difference in their lives by being genuinely compassionate and concerned.*

JACKIE HARTMANN, HUMAN RESOURCES DIRECTOR

*Be an active listener...the best ideas are often overlooked because of either listening only to those, who, by title, is a leader or because you are too focused on what you plan to say. I never learned anything while I was talking.*

*Don't ask others to do what you are not willing to do. Too many leaders lead from a distance. The most effective way to lead is through participation. Respect as a leader is earned most quickly by a willingness to share the workload. As a theme park leader, I would often carry a pan and broom, thereby demonstrating my commitment to the team and job through active participation.*

*The smartest person in the room is often not the sharpest knife in the drawer. Leaders who create a distinct culture of inclusiveness will win in two ways; first by not creating a culture where everyone is waiting on the answer but instead feels empowered to seek the best path forward, secondly by demonstrating humility.*

DONNIE MILLS, FORMER COO AND PARK PRESIDENT—SEAWORLD ORLANDO, DISCOVERY COVE, AQUATICA

*This straightforward business philosophy could be the key to business success as well as personal relationships. The philosophy is so simple that it can be summarized in two words containing eleven letters—No Surprises. No one wants to be blindsided, especially if the news is bad. For people working for you, it's a meaningful discussion to have right away and set the parameters for proper communications. Err on the side of "over-communicating," that way the information is continuously flowing. Never blindside your boss—it could cost your job and career. When establishing an honest, forthcoming relationship based on trust with a spouse, significant other or friends, the "No Surprise" rule will be the foundation for getting along well.*

*Respect and honor those serving and who have served in the military. These volunteers sacrifice much for protecting you and the freedoms we have. Please don't take them for granted. Consider hiring a military vet. Their tremendous skills, such as personal accountability, dedication, and discipline, are all wonderful attributes. As for all the homeless vets, hold the criticism, and show them love and compassion. They deserve it.*

JOSEPH R. SCHILLACI, FORMER CHAIRMAN, PRESIDENT/ CEO, THE FREMONT STREET EXPERIENCE, LAS VEGAS

*Leadership has its own lifespan. You begin by realizing you have skills that work together and somehow, allow you to be heard. Then you move to find work or subjects where you can lend your skills to make a positive change while amassing more subject matter information, data, and understanding. Suddenly, it can feel very lonely—because some decisions create necessary angst and upset the status quo.*

*In the latter stage of maturity, you understand that if you are humane, behaving with sincere interest and love for the person or ideal—you will come through with respect.*

*Also, for leaders, this is the goal: to be fair, humane, honorable, and respectful in the process.*

LISA BROCK, OWNER AND PRESIDENT,
BROCK COMMUNICATIONS

*Life is just wonderful. You have so much to learn and so much to give. Here are a few takeaways I have imparted on my children and friends. Hey, and don't forget, consider all the factors involved:*

*Happiness is a matter of choice. If you don't like where you are, do something about it. It is OK to be a critic, but only if you have a better solution. Learn to be an advocate for a position and not just a naysayer.*

*A sense of humor is vital. A spoon on your nose is worth two in the drawer. Laugh—but only with people, never at them. Follow your ABC's—Always Be Curious. If you don't know, ask. Learn something new every day. When you stop learning, you start to die.*

*You must always be as interested in gaining knowledge as in spreading it. Prepare to listen, to probe and observe the people you meet. Listen carefully, and you will have the advantage. Remember to thank everyone who helped you when you accomplish your goals. Two words to remember and use often—"Please" and "Thank You."*

*You say your job is hard—it is supposed to be! If it were easy, they would have hired some high school kids to do it.*

T. LANDON SMITH, CHAIRMAN AND FOUNDER OF LANG & SMITH ADVERTISING, LTJG US NAVY, EXECUTIVE OFFICER, USS STRINGHAM (DD-83), WWII (1944-1945) (RETIRED)

*Many people spend considerable time on various pursuits to understand and become better at leadership only to fail to achieve success with their teams.*

*What makes the difference between believing in a leader and having a boss? Being ready to grasp moments of truth is essential to show you are a person to be followed.*

*Opportunities to demonstrate your leadership, to 'walk the walk' won't occur every day. Too often, a busy person fails to recognize opportunities to show team integrity, honesty, and a willingness to do hard things. Instead, they may fail to act or shy away from displaying good leadership. It would be best if you can be seen as a leader to be followed. Each moment of truth is an opportunity to be a leader.*

JEFF THEERMAN PE, VICE PRESIDENT, SENIOR UTILITY PERFORMANCE CONSULTANT, BROWN AND CALDWELL, ST. LOUIS

*First, there is an adage that I find especially helpful to young leaders, "When you are through learning, you are through." I frequently talk to MBA students about starting their careers, and I encourage them to cultivate an attitude of curiosity toward business, technology, world politics, and relationships. Ask lots of questions. Wonder why? Read, read, read. Find mentors and other business colleagues that have differing opinions. Use the "tell me more" approach from Covey to dig deeper into others' views.*

*Second, my father-in-law, who was a longtime successful Xerox sales executive, often told me, "It never hurts by hiring smarter people than you are" rather than being replaced by a superstar. His promotions were due to his track record of hiring high potentials. The ability to attract, retain, and engage a top-performing workforce/team is the essence of leadership success. When hire smart is not SOP, you will find that "B" players tend to hire "C" talent, which in turn hire "D" talent. I read once that Silicon Valley, which requires a steady stream of brilliant, creative, flexible talent to keep pace with its incredible technology curve, calls this scenario the "Bozo Spiral." They say that Bozo's are responsible for killing many great business ventures.*

DOUGLAS RAU, FORMER CHRO,
SIGMA-ALDRICH CORPORATION

*Leaders quickly learn the impact organizational culture has on team performance, but they don't always determine how they impact that culture. Try looking in the mirror first. Engage in a personal 360-degree review.*

*Create a comfortable environment. Foster a workplace where individuals can take a risk and make mistakes without fear, and an environment where they can't wait to return each day.*

*Take ownership and don't blame the system or anyone else. Treat each person with respect. Respect is earned. Earn it through your tireless commitment to a healthy, fun environment. Your team will thank you.*

DANIEL BROWN, THEME PARK COO, RETIRED

*Never in your leadership make life difficult for others. Instead, be a source of animation and affirmation. Show them rather than tell them. Think out of the box. Lead by example, especially in developing the culture of change.*

*Be willing to take chances and learn to be comfortable outside of your comfort zone—the magic happens there. Be gracious, yet firm in making decisions done with proper consultation and discernment and think of the best and worst scenario of such choices.*

*Share your leadership of service by recognizing and training future leaders and giving them opportunities to lead. In confronting problems, face them as challenges to be turned into opportunities. Best lessons are not learned from triumphs, but instead from defeats.*

*Remember your awesome responsibility in going about doing God's work. God is always ahead of you in your journey. Trust in him, as nothing is impossible with God.*

JEFFERSON S. BUENVIAJE, MSBA-HRM, DIRECTOR, CENTER FOR STUDENT ADMISSIONS, FORMER DEAN, COLLEGE OF TOURISM & HOSPITALITY MANAGEMENT, DE LA SALLE UNIVERSITY—DASMARIÑAS, DASMARIÑAS CITY, CAVITE, PHILIPPINES

*Everything I learned in life, I learned from others or by making a mistake. There is learning in all your life's experiences. Find a mentor and help your direct reports to find theirs. Read—it can be fiction or nonfiction, self-help, or industry updates. A good leader never, ever, ever stops caring about his team. It is essential to know that you are always on stage. Your team, subordinates, and counterparts are still watching what you do, what you say, and what you fail to do. Act swiftly in addressing a lack of performance.*

*Performance issues fall into two basic categories: knowledge and behavior. Knowledge issues are addressed thru training and mentoring. Behavior issues can be a whole different challenge. Include human resources in any "behavior" discussions as there may be security or legal issues attached to the remedy.*

JACK LAWLER, INDEPENDENT BUSINESS DEVELOPMENT AND ACCOUNT MANAGEMENT CONSULTANT, SPECIALIZING IN FOODSERVICE DISTRIBUTION MANAGEMENT

*Responsibility and authority pertain to scope—functional oversight. In comparison, leadership is not about getting people to fall in line behind a set of organizational mandates. Instead, it's about getting people to join you. The critical measure of an impactful leader is their ability to visibly validate the importance of the intellectual and physical contributions of his or her team.*

*High-impact leaders are never artificial but artful in the ability to provide clarity and execution. Successful leadership stays focused on the key actions which will drive the most critical outcomes. Leaders are masters of the language of action.*

ROI L. EWELL, PRINCIPAL WITH EWELL AND ASSOCIATES

*Leadership is based on trust and respect. Hard to earn, easy to lose. Respect is a two-way street. You desire respect and trust, but you must be willing to show it in return, to those you work with and have business dealings. There will be times during your career when you will need to make a business decision based on this simple principle.*

CY WOODROME, PRESIDENT, MOBILIS HEALTH, LLC

*I always believed my job was to assemble a group of ladies and gentlemen to carry out our goals once our Corporate Board established them. Each person was assigned their individual goals. They were monitored for their progress through weekly and monthly reviews and offer help where needed. I think the best tool to use for leadership is, to be honest, and have the highest integrity. Always be consistent in one's goals and performance as it applies to the action plan of your operation.*

*Finally, always have a management group that believes in a TEAM approach to reach maximum results.*

LARRY B. COCHRAN, SIX FLAGS, CEO, RETIRED

*Authentic leadership, at its core, is simple. Authentic leadership comes from character. Do you remember the fast quips that your Mom, Dad, mentor, teacher, or coach would throw at you? At times, you would wonder what they meant, or would even think, "Wow, they are crazy!" Only to realize years later, "I should have listened more," and spent time learning life lessons from their wisdom.*

*My wife has a great life lesson she learned as a young practicing attorney, that you would find helpful in your leadership journey:*

*Pigs Get Fat. Hogs Get Slaughtered.*

*This idiom is easy to apply to your leadership journey! Are you always a "taker"—or the person trying to get too much out of a situation—deal or people? Ask yourself, are you about serving, or about taking? You will find that takers or hogs at some point in their journey will overplay their hand and get burned up or burned out. Pigs or Leaders or Servants have a bigger vision, listen carefully, work with people, and serve a cause bigger than themselves, and tend to have much longer careers. I would encourage you to look at leadership as a long journey and serve.*

JAY GALBRAITH, VALENCIA COLLEGE,
VP OF PUBLIC AFFAIRS

*Passion, passion, passion, along with a good dose of common sense and creativity, have been the keys to my success. Serving as the Outdoor Amusement Business Association, a national trade association for over 50 years, our Board of Directors are mostly generation, family business leaders, whose forefathers and mothers began building their businesses with America's fairs and festivals three to four generations before them. The newer generation is better educated, knows how to utilize social media and metrics to build their businesses and to operate more efficiently. While this is still a labor-intensive industry, training their people and building relationships with their event sponsors, rely on their vision and passion and enthusiasm to succeed. When dealing with board members or business owners, getting them to focus on the future, and not just put out fires in their daily operation, requires a lot of passion and creativity to raise the bar even higher for the good of our industry.*

*It's a top-down business philosophy that trickles down to the lowest level employee to keep them motivated and challenged every single day. I look for Board members who have these same values and are in it for the long haul and the next generation of showmen and ladies.*

ROBERT W. JOHNSON, PAST PRESIDENT/CEO,
OUTDOOR AMUSEMENT BUSINESS ASSOCIATION, INC.

*The powerful lesson I'd like to share is that leadership is a balancing act. For companies to be successful, they must keep customers, shareholders, and employees happy. The leader's job is to juggle the needs and desires of all three and make decisions to help achieve each group's goals. The best leaders are the ones good at juggling!*

KEITH ALPER, CEO, NITROUS EFFECT, AUTHOR OF *FROM LIKE TO LOVE: INSPIRING EMOTIONAL COMMITMENT FROM EMPLOYEES AND CUSTOMERS*

*My career started at Walt Disney World at the Magic Kingdom ticket gate. I worked my way up to being on the team that created the Disney Institute. The Institute shared the Disney Approach to People, Management, and Service to people and companies around the world. I have worked with many great brands and companies, but at the end of the day, my top 4 greatest leadership lessons came from Mickey Mouse!*

*#1 Remind people they make a difference no matter what their role is in the company—it takes everyone together to make magic!*

*#2 Step into your customer's shoes; ask them, listen to them, and evaluate your business from their experience. Their experience should drive all that you do!*

*#3 If employees know they matter and enjoy working for you, THEN they will pass that on to customers! Like a chain of dominoes—what happens on the inside spills out to the customer!*

*#4 And don't forget to add the "Pixie Dust!" Where can you add something unexpected; something that makes them say WOW? When employees and customers walk out the door—or get off the phone, they say something about you. Make sure both the customer and the employee are saying what you want them to and doing the marketing for you!*

SUSIE PECUCH, OWNER/CONSULTANT /SPEAKER,
DESIGN THE CUSTOMER CONVERSATION

*There's right, and there's wrong. You got to do one thing or the other. You do the one, and you're living. You do the other, and you may be walking around, but you're dead as a beaver hat.*

DAVY CROCKETT, AS PLAYED BY JOHN WAYNE IN THE 1960 MOVIE, *THE ALAMO*

# EPILOGUE

## CONTINUE YOUR JOURNEY

*To get through the hardest journey, you need to take only one step at a time, but you must keep on stepping.*

—CHINESE PROVERB

*This is your journey, your body, your mind, and your spirit. Dig deep, own it, and start doing things for you and by you.*

—ANONYMOUS

*Life is a journey where you make choices. Make good ones, be better, smile often.*

—GARY VIEN

Thank you for your time in reading this book on leadership. It has been an incredible journey for me, and I hope it has been for you as well.

Looking back through my Little Brown Journal, I found some additional writings which I enjoyed and helped me on my path. I hope to continue to feed your curiosity and that you see new insights and ideas to think about as you walk your leadership journey. Never stop journaling those things which you want to remember and use in the future.

It would be best if you continued to challenge yourself through education. Once you have it, no man can take it away from you, and it is your responsibility to use it.

### A NOTE TO A FRIEND ON HER PROMOTION—

First—Remember from whence you came. All the employees are looking to you to be their advocate and support. They need guidance, assistance, and at some point in time, a little shove. Think of their perspective when decision times come.

Second—Spend time to think and to listen. You are the one with the vision, and as the new leader, you must project that in all instances. It doesn't mean you have all the answers or exactly know where you are going all the time, but you must show some courage and fortitude when it comes time for decisions. Most, if not all, will line up behind you. The department is yours to mold and grow. Listen to the ones doing the work. Think about how you can support them and make their lives easier. If you don't do this, who will?

Third—Have fun. Life will never be the same again. Your attitude and how you approach the job are within your control—use it wisely. You will have to grow two-inch-thick skin to take all the torpedoes coming your way. Nothing is personal—this is work; this is business. If you don't drive the train—they will. Enjoy your work, but work is not everything. Family comes first. Smile a lot—it keeps people wondering.

### TAKE ANOTHER ENGLISH COURSE

My father used this direction with all of my brothers and sisters, and I have vowed that I, too, will use it on my children.

I never liked the words. They seem to be a put down every time I mispronounced a word or used incorrect English. One day after I completed my second year in college, Dad and I went fishing, and I mustered up enough courage to ask why he repeatedly said to each of his children, "Take another English course."

As some fathers do, he responded not with a simple one-phrase explanation, but rather a short dissertation on the necessity to use proper English, correct spelling, proper grammar, and crisp pronunciation.

"Employers will note these things on future applications, resumes, and interviews," he said, "and every organization needs people who know how to write and speak correctly."

All these thoughts made sense to me, but he really made his point and drove it home some years later, when half in jest and half prophetically he said, "Who knows? Someday you may want to write a book!"

All the best of luck and success in whatever role you find yourself in—keep learning and keep leading!

Gary

# ABOUT THE AUTHOR

**GARY VIEN** is an eternal optimist, finding lessons in leadership everywhere he looks. He has been fortunate to work throughout the United States in the entertainment industry as a senior leader for almost forty years and has recruited internationally. He then found additional purpose and opportunities within the credit union movement. Vien serves on many community and national volunteer boards in various executive and leadership positions.

These experiences have deepened his passion and drive to focus on developing leadership skills to help young professionals and emerging new leaders reach their potential and to use their expertise to make their communities better.

**www.GaryVien.com**